ARCHITECTURE AND URBANISM
2022:10 No.625

発行者
吉田信之

チーフ・エディトリアル・アドヴァイザー
セン・クアン

ゲスト・エディター
木村博昭

副編集長
佐藤綾子

編集
シルビア・チェン（シンガポール）
アメナ・ラマン
岩淵美月

レイアウト制作
安藤聡（pickles design）

編集委員
バリー・バーグドール
ジョヴァンナ・ボラーシ
アンドレス・レピック

顧問
寺松康裕

デザイン
マッシモ・ヴィネリ

©建築と都市　625号　令和4年9月27日発行
毎月1回27日発行
昭和46年3月3日第三種郵便物認可
定価：2,852円（本体2,593円）
年間購読料34,224円（年12冊／税・送料込み）
発行：株式会社エー・アンド・ユー
〒100-6017　東京都千代田区霞が関三丁目2番5号霞が関ビルディング17階
電話：(03)6205-4384　FAX：(03)6205-4387
青山ハウス
〒107-0062　東京都港区南青山二丁目19番14号
電話：(03)6455-5597　FAX：(03)6455-5583
E-mail: au@japan-architect.co.jp
URL: https://japan-architect.co.jp
振替：00130-5-98119
印刷：大日本印刷株式会社
取次店＝トーハン・日販・中央社・鍬谷・西村・楽天ブックスネットワーク

特集：
チャールズ・レニー・マッキントッシュ

エッセイ：
工芸的思考：マッキントッシュのトータルデザイン　5
木村博昭

住宅

ヒル・ハウス　12

エッセイ：
住宅のための仮設住宅　50
アンディ・グローク

ウィンディ・ヒル　58

芸術愛好家の家　66

芸術家の田園住宅と都市住宅、オーチェンボシーのゲート・ロッジ　72

インテリア

マッキントッシュ自邸　76

ハウス・ヒル　88

ウィロー・ティールーム　92

ブキャナン・ストリート・ティールーム　104

アーガイル・ストリート・ティールーム　106

イングラム・ストリート・ティールーム　107

78ダンゲート　110

公共建築

グラスゴー美術学校　116

エッセイ：
感情よりも状況を：火災が明らかにしたもの　152
サリー・スチュアート

グラスゴー・ヘラルド　156

クイーンズ・クロス教会　158

スコットランド・ストリート・スクール　162

表紙：「ヒル・ハウス」。
裏表紙：「ブキャナン・ストリート・ティールーム」。

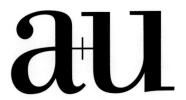

ARCHITECTURE AND URBANISM
2022:10   No.625

Publisher:
Nobuyuki Yoshida

Chief Editorial Advisor:
Seng Kuan

Guest Editor:
Hiroaki Kimura

Senior Editor:
Ayako Sato

Editors:
Sylvia Chen (Singapore)
Amena Rahman
Mizuki Iwabuchi

Layout:
Satoshi Ando (pickles design)

Copyeditor:
Amy Teschner

Editorial Board:
Barry Bergdoll
Giovanna Borasi
Andres Lepik

Consultant:
Yasuhiro Teramatsu

Design:
Massimo Vignelli

Distributor:
Shinkenchiku-sha Co., Ltd.

©A+U Publishing Co., Ltd. 2022
Printed in Japan
Published by A+U Publishing Co., Ltd.
Kasumigaseki Building 17F, 3-2-5,
Kasumigaseki, Chiyoda-ku, Tokyo
100-6017, Japan
Tel: +81-3-6205-4384 Fax: +81-3-6205-4387
Aoyama House
2-19-14 Minamiaoyama, Minato-ku, Tokyo
107-0062, Japan
Tel: +81-3-6455-5597 Fax: +81-3-6455-5583
Email: au@japan-architect.co.jp
URL: https://au-magazine.com

ISBN 978-4-9002-1282-4
a+u = Architecture and Urbanism is handled
exclusively
by Shinkenchiku-sha Co., Ltd.:
Kasumigaseki Building 17F, 3-2-5,
Kasumigaseki, Chiyoda-ku, Tokyo
100-6017, Japan
Tel: +81-3-6205-4380 Fax: +81-3-6205-4386
Email: ja-business@japan-architect.co.jp
Subscription rate for 2022 outside Japan
¥42,000 (Airmail – Asia), ¥45,000 (Airmail –
Europe, North America, Oceania, & Middle
East), ¥49,000 (Airmail – South America &
Africa)
US Dollars, Euro, and Sterling Pounds
equivalent to the above Japanese Yen prices are
acceptable. When you remit, please convert to
the current exchange rate.

Feature:
Charles Rennie Mackintosh

Essay:
The Philosophy of Craft:
The Total Design of Charles Rennie Mackintosh   5
Hiroaki Kimura

Houses

The Hill House   12
Essay:
A Temporary House for a House   50
Andy Groarke

Windy Hill   58

House for an Art Lover   66

Artist's House in the Country and Town, and Gate Lodge at
Auchenbothie   72

Interiors

Mackintosh House   76

Hous'hill   88

Willow Tea Rooms   92

Buchanan Street Tea Rooms   104

Argyle Street Tea Rooms   106

Ingram Street Tea Rooms   107

78 Derngate   110

Public Buildings

Glasgow School of Art   116
Essay:
More Conditions than Sentiments: Revealed by Fire   152
Sally Stewart

Glasgow Herald   156

Queen's Cross Church   158

Scotland Street School   162

Front cover: The Hill House. Photo by Johan Dehlin, courtesy of Carmody Groarke.
Back cover: Buchanan Street Tea Rooms. Photo courtesy of T. & R. Annan and Sons.

Feature:
Charles Rennie Mackintosh

特集：
チャールズ・レニー・マッキントッシュ

a+u's October issue features the work of Charles Rennie Mackintosh, born in 1868, in Glasgow, Scotland. Glasgow grew rapidly into a modern industrialized city in the latter half of the 1800s. With this urban development came a generation of students from Glasgow School of Art, including Mackintosh and his close associates known as The Four, who started creating designs and artworks from an entirely new vantage point. As detailed in an essay by guest editor Hiroaki Kimura, Mackintosh enriched traditional architectural composition through his advocacy of the "philosophy of craft," which brought together craft and engineering. In their distance from historicist styles and pursuit of a new environmental aesthetic, these activities paralleled other movements in continental Europe at the turn of the 20th century. This issue showcases 15 built works by Mackintosh through lavish displays of archival drawings and historical photographs. The themes of conservation and preservation are paramount in considering the legacy of Mackintosh, as highlighted in the sheltering of Hill House and coming to terms with the loss of the Glasgow School of Art building. (*a+u*)

『a+u』10月号はチャールズ・レニー・マッキントッシュの建築作品を特集する。マッキントッシュは1868年スコットランド、グラスゴーに生まれる。19世紀後半はちょうどグラスゴーが工業化にともなって近代工業都市として急速に発展した時期である。この都市の発展にともなって、マッキントッシュや彼の仲間ザ・フォーなどグラスゴー美術学校で学んだ世代によってまったく新たな立脚点を発したデザインや芸術品が生みだされた。マッキントッシュは、特集のゲストエディター木村博昭が指摘するような「工芸的思考」をもって、工芸とエンジニアリングを分けることなく、伝統的な建築構成の領域を拡大した。これまでの様式建築から離れその地に応じた美学を生みだそうという動きは、大陸欧州におけるほかの芸術運動との並行していた。本特集ではマッキントッシュによる実作15作をとり上げ、アーカイヴ図面や当時の写真などとともに紹介する。また、ヒル・ハウスのシェルター建設とグラスゴー美術学校建物の喪失を受け入れること、二つの事象を通し現代におけるマッキントッシュ建築にとって重要な保全と保存の問題をとり上げる。（編）

Charles Rennie Mackintosh (1868–1928)

1868 Born on June 7, in Glasgow, an industrial city in Scotland, United Kingdom.
1884 Aspiring to be an architect, he studies under architect John Hutchinson. That same year, he enrolls at Glasgow School of Art and settles into a life of work in both architecture and fine art.
1889 Joins the firm of John Honeyman and John Keppie, and works there for the next 25 years.
1900 Marries artist Margaret Macdonald on August 22.
1902 Joins the firm as a partner. The firm is renamed Honeyman, Keppie and Mackintosh.
1913 His partnership in the firm of Honeyman, Keppie and Mackintosh is dissolved.
1915 Moves to London to work in his studio.
1923 Completely withdraws from architectural work and devotes himself to watercolor painting in Port-Vendres, south of France.
1928 Dies of tongue cancer on December 10, in London.

チャールズ・レニー・マッキントッシュ（1868〜1928）

1868 英国スコットランドの工業都市グラスゴーに生まれる。
1884 建築家を目指し始める。建築家ジョン・ハチソンに師事。同年グラスゴー美術学校に入籍。
1889 ジョン・ハニマン・アンド・ケペ事務所に移籍。以降25年間同事務所で活動。
1900 8月22日アーティストのマーガレット・マクドナルドと結婚。
1902 ハニマン・アンド・ケペ事務所パートナーに加わる。ハニマン・ケペアンドマッキントッシュ事務所と改称。
1913 ハニマン・ケペ・アンド・マッキントッシュ事務所のパートナーを解消。
1915 ロンドンに移居しアトリエで活動する。
1923 以降、建築の仕事から完全に離れ、南仏ポール＝ヴァンドルで水彩画に専念。
1928 癌に冒され、12月10日生涯を終える。

Project descriptions by Hiroaki Kimura.／作品解説：木村博昭
Editorial support from Kanae Yoshimura.／編集協力：吉村香苗

Essay:
The Philosophy of Craft: The Total Design of Charles Rennie Mackintosh
Hiroaki Kimura

エッセイ：
工芸的思考：マッキントッシュのトータルデザイン
木村博昭

The Beginning – and End – of Modernism

I began studying architecture in the 1970s, during the generation of Expo '70 in Osaka, Japan. This was supposed to be the era of late modernism, but half a century later, it seems to me that we are still towing the line of modernism. The premodern era of art nouveau and art deco was short-lived, lasting only 30 years or so, and was swept away after World War I at the beginning of the 20th century, when modernism began. Charles Rennie Mackintosh was a premodern architect who, in response to social changes brought about by the technological innovations of the end of the 19th century, sought to move on from a previous era of architecture based on style, and toward modernism. This modernism began in Glasgow, Scotland, in the far north of Europe. To decipher the sources, ideas, and vectors associated with the architects who created the new architecture that Mackintosh aspired to, as well as the methods they embodied, is for us a reevaluation of modernism. Today, we are in a similar position, during an era of dramatic transformation due to shifts in the industrial structure of AI (artificial intelligence) and digitization.

I have visited Maison Louis Carré, the 1959 house designed by Alvar and Elissa Aalto in the suburbs of Versailles, France, several times. The sloping roofs that line up next to each other according to the gradient of the site; the large undulating wooden ceiling in the hall; the gentle staircase leading down to the sunken living room it is continuous with; the interior, furniture, and lighting; the delicate and meticulous detailing; and the garden and landscape that connect the inside and outside – all of these elements are part of Aalto's world. Nothing is prefabricated. Sitting in the sofa chair and gazing at the interior and outside give one a pleasant sensation and a sense of calm and security, conveyed, moreover, in terms of a timeless spatial experience, a feeling of emotional excitement and coziness, thanks to Aalto's unique sense of the modern world. Architecture is an offering made to a specific place and client, a one-of-a-kind entity that exists only where it does, and Maison Louis Carré reminded me of the importance of this singularity. Café Aalto, located in the bookstore of the Stockman department store in Helsinki, is another space that, while not singular, felt safe and comfortable. These experiences overlap with the comfortable spaces I experienced at Mackintosh's The Hill House (pp. 12–49) and Willow Tea Rooms (pp. 92–103).

The architectural form of modernism has shifted from the era of stone architecture and spaces carved out of mass, which followed a continuous, unbroken lineage from the classical style of architecture, to an age where this volume of space itself is

モダニズム、始まりと終わり

私自身が建築を学び始めたのは70年代、Expo' 70の世代である。後期モダニズムの時代と言われた時代であるが、半世紀を経た現在も未だモダニズムの線上に立ち止まったままに思える。プレモダンであったアール・ヌーボー、アール・デコの激変の時代は、たった30年余りの短命に終わり、第一次世界大戦後、20世紀初頭には一掃されモダニズムが始まった。マッキントッシュは、19世紀末の技術革新を転機とした社会変革にともない、それまでの様式建築からモダニズムを目指したプレモダンの建築家である。モダニズムは、欧州の最も外れにある北国スコットランドのグラスゴーから始まった。マッキントッシュが求めていた、新たな建築が創造されて行く建築家の源泉や考え方、そのベクトル、具現化したその手法を読みとくことは、我々にとってのモダニズムの再考でもあり、また、AIやデジタル化の産業構造の変化に伴う著しい変革の現代にあって、我々も同様な立場にある。

何度かベルサイユ郊外にあるアルヴァ、エリッサ・アアルトによる住宅、カレ邸を訪れた事がある。傾斜敷地に合わせて雁行した傾斜屋根、ホールはアアルト特有の大きくうねる木製のシーリング、そこから緩やかな階段を下り、沈み込むようなリヴィングへと連続した空間、そのインテリアと家具と照明、繊細で隅々まで配慮されたディテール、そして、内と外が繋がる庭園とのランドスケープに至るまで、すべてはアアルトの世界である。既製品は何もない。ソファー椅子に腰掛け、インテリアと外を眺めると、心地よい感触と穏やかな安心感が漂う。時間を超えた空間体験として伝わり、彼の固有の世界感を通して、感動と居心地のよさを感じたのである。建築は特定の場所とクライアントにたいするものであり、唯一無二の存在であり、この固有の重要さを再確認させられたのである。ヘルシンキのストックマンのブックカフェも、特異ではないが安心感と心地よさを感じた空間である。マッキントッシュのヒル・ハウス（12～49頁）やウィロー・ティールーム（92～103頁）で体験した心地よい空間と重なる。

モダニズムにあって、コンクリート・鉄・ガラスの建築素材や構造、そして量産化の革新的技術によって、これまでの古典様式建築から脈々と継続されていた石造のマッスから削り得た空間の時代は、空間そのもののヴォリュームを操作する時代に変わり、これまでの建築空間の概念は変化し、飛躍的な展開を遂げる。しかし、実はモダニズムの建築家が目指したものは、建築技術の飛躍による新建築の空間のみならず、最も重要であるのは、人に寄り添う空間の創造であり、アアルトの建築のような、そして、マッキントッシュのヒル・ハウスやウィロー・ティールームで体験した、心地よい感触と安心感に満ちた空間ではなかろうか。人には、それぞれに世界感があり個性がある。そして、人は人に接して、個々の世界感を理解し、共感や心地よさを得る、唯一無二の存在である事を理解している。建築も然り、人を対象に、そこにしか存在しない世界感の空間を提示する、唯一無二のものである。モダニズム建築は、観念的な空間操作をする一方で、社会そして

manipulated, through materials and structures of concrete, steel, and glass, as well as innovative technologies for mass production. This dramatic development brought about a conceptual change in previous architectural space. In fact, what modernist architects were aiming for was not only new architectural space created by dramatic improvements in building technologies, but also, most importantly, comfortable spaces for people to inhabit, as seen in the architecture of Aalto and the sort of comfort and security one experiences in Mackintosh's The Hill House and Willow Tea Rooms. Each person has their own sense of the world and individuality. Moreover, people understand that they are the only ones who can comprehend their individual sense of the world, and they feel empathy and comfort by interacting with others. Architecture, too, is a singular thing, presenting a space with a human sense of the world that could only exist in that locale. Modernist architecture, on the other hand, is a conceptual or ideological manipulation of space: it was created in the context of society and life as a whole, based on the ideal of a space that feels initmate.

Total Design and Integrated Aesthetic Space
Evaluations of architecture often mention the terms "Mackintosh style" and "Wright style," for example. While ambiguous, these descriptors indicate something about the uniqueness of the building in question. Without a certain distinct, named character, these too would be mere inorganic, universal spaces. Naturally, architectural details are strong expressions of the uniqueness of the designer that demonstrate specific, concrete characteristics.

Mackintosh's architecture possesses aesthetic harmony; its spaces seek out a sense of unity between the architecture itself, the landscape, the interior, the furniture, the art, and the delicate details created by the craftspeople. These spaces act on the senses that relate to human touch, just as craft does. This is an important determinant of the kind of comfort that goes beyond functionality, and it resonates with our soul and senses. As a result, Mackintosh's charm and appeal lie in this ideal style of fastidiousness and purity in design. The practical realization of Mackintosh's ideal expression of space, after all, began with a series of private client residences exemplified by Hill House, built at the beginning of the 20th century, or the familiar living spaces of Miss Cranston's Tea Rooms (pp. 92–109), cafés for people to gather that were effectively a kind of commons, before he moved on to put his stamp on spaces of perfect aesthetic harmony with his brilliant, total designs.

I have learned that architecture, as a kind of moral code of modernism, should possess a single continuity in its form, structure, and every detail, from the design of the doorknob to the furniture and architectural detailing. Certainly, this is where the uniqueness and fastidious purity of architecture manifests itself. Today, there are myriad standardized products marketed for performance, price, and safety, and a thousand different choices and combinations are possible. We find ourselves selecting standard products and combinations thereof, and it would be irrational to refuse to use these standardized items. Even if their performance could be guaranteed, however, it follows quite naturally that the uniqueness of the architecture in question would suffer.

Mass production also rejects substandard products, or those where productivity is low. Conversely, there is a sense of trustworthiness and security when it comes to objects or crafts where the designer or creator can be readily identified. For sustainable development goals (SDGs), high-quality crafts produced in small quantities have an advantage over mass-produced products that involve greater environmental impact. The warmth and simplicity of handmade craftsmanship, which cannot be experienced with standardized products or manufactured goods, is seen as a virtue, and the way that people interact with things is being reconsidered. This situation recalls the period that brought about the Arts and Crafts movement, which led to the Bauhaus, and the period when John Ruskin established some sort of moral standard for architecture, which entailed the creation of beauty through handicraft. The beginning of this practice was the Arts and Crafts that came after William Morris, the spirit of which was then carried forward by Mackintosh, who together with Josef Hoffmann and others of the Vienna Secession, perfected a world of ideal aesthetic spaces connected to daily life. A continuous, integrated space that encompassed furniture and interior design along with architecture, which was subsequently espoused by the Bauhaus as well giants of modernism such as Ludwig Mies van der Rohe, Le Corbusier, Frank Lloyd Wright, and Alvar Aalto, became an important characteristic of modernist architecture.

The Glasgow Four: The Formation of Designer Groups
James Herbert MacNair (1868–1955) attended classes with Mackintosh at the Glasgow School of Art, and the 2 of them were colleagues at the architectural firm Honeyman and Keppie. Starting around 1894, they formed a creative group called The Glasgow Four, a quartet of 2 architects (himself and Mackintosh) and 2 artists, sisters Margaret (1864–1933) and Frances MacDonald (1873–1921). Later, Herbert and Frances married in 1899, while Charles and Margaret married the following year.

Although The Glasgow Four were committed to the Arts and Crafts style, which prized the texture of materials, starting in 1898 MacNair took up an instructor position at University College, Liverpool, and the work of the Four was passed on to Charles and Margaret, who promoted a semi-industrialized approach that eradicated all sense of materiality in a departure from Arts and Crafts. Using white, black, and silver colors, they

生活に総合的にかかわる中で創造され、親密な空間を理想としたと思える。

トータルデザインと一体的美的空間
建築を評するとき、たとえば、マッキントッシュ風、ライト風などと言われ、曖昧ながらもその建築の固有性を示している。これらも「らしさ」を除けばただの無機質なユニバーサル空間になってしまう。当然、建築のディテールは、設計者の固有性が強く表現されたものであり、具体的な特性を示すものである。

マッキントッシュの建築は、建築自体とランドスケープ・インテリア・家具・芸術・職人による繊細なディテールなど、工芸のように人に最も近い部分の感覚に作用する、一体性を追求した美的調和の空間である。それが、機能性を越えた、魂や感性に響く心地よさを決定する重要な要素であろう。結果としてもたらされたデザインにたいする潔癖性と純粋性の理想的な作風がマッキントッシュの魅力である。マッキントッシュの理想的空間表現が実践できたのは、やはり最初は、20世紀初頭のヒル・ハウスに代表される個人クライアントの住宅であり、また、市民が集うコモンとなるカフェである一連のクランストン・ティールーム（92〜109頁）の身近な生活空間であった。ここでマッキントッシュは見事にトータル・デザインによる完璧な美的調和の空間を完成させた。

モダニズムの道徳的規範として、建築は、その形態・構造、そしてドアノブのデザインから家具・ディテールの隅々まで一つの連続性があるべきと私は学んだ。確かに、そこに建築の固有性と潔癖な純粋性が生まれる。現在は、性能・価格・安全性から見ても、多種多様な規格のプロダクトがあり、千差万別の選択や組み合わせが可能な時代である。気づけば、規格品の選択や組み合わせの選択を行っている。規格品の使用を拒む事は、かえって不合理でもある。ただ、性能は保証出来ても、その結果建築の固有性が薄れて行くのは当然である。

そして、量産化は規格外や生産性の悪いものを否定する。一方、デザイナーや制作者の顔が見えるもの、工芸品にはその信頼と安心感がある。SDGsの視点からしても、環境負荷をともなう大量生産プロダクトより、少量生産・高品質の工芸品が優位である。また規格品やプロダクト製品では味わえない手工の温もりや素朴さが美徳とされ、ものと人とのかかわり方が再考されている。これは、かつてのアーツ・アンド・クラフツ運動のきっかけと成り、バウハウスに繋がる、ジョン・ラスキンが主張した、手工を通して美を創造するという建築の一つの道徳的基準を打ち立てた時代にも似ている。そして、その実践は、ウィリアム・モリス以後のアーツ・アンド・クラフツに始まり、マッキントッシュに受け継がれ、生活と繋がる理想的な美的空間の世界をウィーン派のホフマン達と共に完成させた。その後、バウハウスおよびモダニズムの巨匠達、ミース、コルビュジエ、ライト、アアルトなどの建築家に受け継がれ、建築と共に、家具・インテリアの連続的な一体空間の重要性は、モダニズム建築の重要な特質となった。

ザ・フォー　デザイナーグループの結成
マッキントッシュとグラスゴー美術学校の仲間であった、ハーバード・マクネイアー（1868〜1955、ジョン・ハニマン・アンド・ケペ建築事務所の同僚）、そして、マーガレットとフランシス・マクドナルド姉妹（1864〜1933、1873〜1921）は、2人の建築家と2人の女性アーティストの男女混成の4人組として、恐らく1894年頃から、「ザ・フォー」と呼ばれた創作グループを組織、活動を始めた。後に、1899年にマクネイアーとフランシスが、そして翌年マッキントッシュとマーガレットが結婚する。

また、ザ・フォーの結成の動機は、モリス・マーシャル・フォークナー商会の設立、アーツ・アンド・クラフツ、そしてイングランドを中心に建築家・デザイナー・職人・アーティスト達が共に連帯したいくつかのグループが結成された工芸運動からの影響と思われる。

ザ・フォーは、材料の素材感を大切にしたアーツ・アンド・クラフツに傾倒していたが、1898年からマクネイアーはリバープル大学に教師として赴任し、4人の活動はマッキントッシュとマーガレットに受け継がれる。アーツ・アンド・クラフツに離反し、半工業化を進めた素材感を消去した、白・黒・シルバーを使い、作風はより幾何学的抽象感を表現した独創的なグラスゴー・スタイルを打ちだしており、彼らはそれまでのアール・ヌーヴォーの領域を拡大した、より伝統に拘らないフリースタイルな展開を示している。

このグラスゴー・スタイルにインスピレーションや影響を及ぼしたであろう、彼らの背景となる、グラスゴー美術大学の学長フランシス・ニューベリー、そして、グラスゴー・ボーイズ（スコットランドの印象派）の存在も、彼らが成熟していく上で重要な役割を担っていたと考えられる。

1900年の第8回ウィーン分離派展への参加、そして、トリノでの現代装飾美術国際展示会（1902年）への参加は、既に大陸でアバンギャルドとして活躍していたグラスゴー・デザイナー達が重要な立場にあった証であり、彼らにとってもヨーロッパでの活動および分離派との結びつきは、大いなる刺激となったはずである。

建築家とデザイナーたちの同盟
デザイナー組織の結成は、19世紀末の特色であろう。ラスキンの工芸への眼差しに始まり、モリスの社会と芸術のかかわり方や、友人の建築家フリップ・ウェブや画家のエドワード・バーン＝ジョーンズ、ダンテ・ゲイブリエル・ロセッティらと共に壁紙や家具を手掛けたモリス・マーシャル・フォークナー商会の設立は、イングランドを中心に若い建築家やデザイナー達に影響を与えた。そしてアーツ・アンド・クラフツ運動へ繋がり、アート・ワーカーズ・ギルドや、チャールズ・ロバート・アシュビーのギルド・オブ・ハンディクラフトなど、建築家・デザイナー・職人・アーティストが連帯したいくつかのグループが結成された。これは恐らく、マッキントッシュとザ・フォーの結成の動機に繋がるだろうし、その後のヨーゼフ・ホフマンとコロマン・モーザー、パトロンのフリッツ・ヴェルンドルファーらによって設立されたウィーン工房に繋がり、そして後には建築・芸術・工芸の関係性を重んじたバウハウスへと引き継がれたと想像できる。

forged a unique Glasgow style with a greater sense of geometric abstraction. In a sense, their work expanded on the art nouveau idiom, and demonstrated the development of a freer style that was not bound by tradition.

The presence of Glasgow School of Art director Francis Henry Newbery, who likely inspired and influenced the Glasgow style, as well as the Glasgow Boys (Scottish Impressionists), also seem to have played an important role in the maturation of these artists.

The participation of Charles and Margaret and their colleagues in the Eighth Exhibition of the Vienna Secession of 1900, and The Glasgow Four in the First International Exhibition of Modern Decorative Arts, held in Turin testified to how the Glasgow designers were already active as the avant-garde on the continent, and the fact that their activities in Europe and their association with the Vienna Secession must have been a great stimulus.

Alliances between Architects and Designers
The formation of organizations or collectives of designers might be said to be a distinctive characteristic of the late 19th century, beginning with Ruskin's attention to craft or Morris's approach to relating art to society. The establishment of Morris, Marshall, Faulkner & Co., which produced wallpaper and furniture together with architect Philip Webb and painters Edward Burne-Jones and Dante Gabriel Rossetti, influenced young architects and designers in England and elsewhere. This led to several groups of architects, designers, craftspeople, and artists to come together in solidarity, as seen in the Arts and Crafts movement, the formation of the Art Workers Guild, and the founding of C. R. Ashbee's Guild and School of Handicraft. These developments may have motivated the formation of The Glasgow Four, as well as the Wiener Werkstätte (Vienna Workshop) which was subsequently established by Josef Hoffmann, Koloman Moser, and arts patron Fritz Waerndorfer, whose spirit seems to have subsequently been inherited by the Bauhaus, thus emphasizing the relationship between architecture, art, and craft.

Mackintosh and Hoffmann were architects who successfully realized their ideals of total design thinking in practice. Their ability to offer artistic relationships and connections and high-quality objects and designs for all aspects of life would not have been possible without the organizations behind the realization of their vision, such as The Glasgow Four, which included women artists, his studio, and kindred students at Glasgow School of Art, and Hoffmann's Wiener Werkstätte. As the transnational alliance between the Hoffmann-led Vienna Secession and The Glasgow Four spread, the previously closed social structure of the traditional master-disciple relationship reconstructed, with this vertical and hierarchical social structure turning into a more democratic, horizontal network through the formation of such alliances. Their thinking and ideals were developed into an international style that was then carried forward by modernism.

The Potential of the Philosophy of Craft
With today's globalization, developments in the architecture world travel and spread at a rapid pace. The values of architects in Europe, Japan, and United States are fairly aligned with each other, and their directions and approaches, too, display little variation. In terms of locality, there is still room for new ideas that go beyond the notion of creation, while in the domain of craft, there is an entire world of climate, tradition, and history unique to each country or region, and unknown to us. During Mackintosh's time, when the craft movement began, the philosophy of craft was an important factor in the process by which modernism took shape. Craft combines practicality and aesthetic value: it represents the inherited experience of tradition and the accumulation of subtle and refined techniques and wisdom. Moreover, as foreseen by the architects of the past, modernism, which transformed values associated with the classical style, began with the inspiration of folk art and craft. Today, as a reaction against excessive industrialization of products, crafts that are well made and durable, tailored to individual needs are again drawing attention. In the future, while we may see a revitalization of the advanced skills of craftspeople, novel ideas and designs are ultimately born and developed through the creativity of craft artists who pursue consummate mastery. Collaborative research and development between crafts and other industries, along with connections between design, science and technology are now global trends.

This reaffirmation of the philosophy of craft is a return to the origins of architecture that have been overlooked by modernism and contemporary architecture. The pursuit of fastidiousness and a purity of design, and the spirituality of the artist and space are perennial human themes that represent the importance and reaffirmation of the sensible values of respect and dignity.

Just as Mackintosh designed everything in his spaces to articulate a world of integral aesthetic harmony, it seems to me that a strong sense of particularity and specific worldviews in architecture will open new possibilities for the field.

Translated by Darryl Jingwen Wee

マッキントッシュとホフマンは、彼らが理想とするトータル・デザイン思想を実践で見事に確立した建築家である。建築家が生活の全般に渡り、そして芸術的なかかわりや高品質な物やデザインを提供出来た背景には、マッキントッシュには女性アーティストの参加するザ・フォーとグラスゴー美術学校の工房や仲間達、そして、ホフマンにはウィーン工房と、彼らの構想の具現化に協力した背後の組織が要因としてあるだろう。また、ホフマン率いるウィーン分離派と、グラスゴーのマッキントッシュらザ・フォーとの、国境を越えた同盟関係の拡がりは、従来の師弟関係で閉ざされた社会構造からはなれ、同盟を結ぶという民主的な横のネットワークに再構築する方法となり、彼らの思想や理念はそのままインターナショナルなスタイルとして展開され、モダニズムに受け継がれたのではないかと思える。

工芸的思考における可能性
現在、グローバル化と共に、世界の建築界で起こり得ることは、速さに伝わり、我々建築家の価値観は欧米や日本で並行し、方向性もさほど変わりはない。ローカリティには、まだ創造を超えて新たな発想をもたらす余地があり、工芸の世界にも、風土・伝統・歴史やその国・地域ならではの我々が知らない世界がある。工芸運動で始まったマッキントッシュの時代とその工芸的思考は、モダニズム形成の重要なファクターであった。工芸は、実用性と美的価値とを兼ね備え、伝統に引き継がれた経験値と、繊細で洗練された技術と知恵の集積である。そして、かつての建築家たちの予感として、民芸や工芸のインスピレーションから、古典様式の価値観を変革したモダニズムは始まった。現代、プロダクトの行き過ぎた工業化にたいする反立として、個別の要求に合わせ、よいもので長く使える工芸品が注目される。職人のもつ高度技能の再現自体は可能かもしれないが、結局のところ、高度な職人技を追求する工芸作家の創造力によって斬新なアイディアやデザインが生まれ、発展がある。工芸と他業種との連携・研究開発、そしてテクノロジー・科学とデザインの結びつきは、世界的潮流でもある。

工芸的思考の再認識は、モダニズム以来現代建築が見落としていた、建築の原点回帰である。デザインの潔癖性や純粋性の追求、作家の精神性と空間は常に人に寄り添うものであり、尊敬や尊厳という感性の価値の重要性と再認識を意味している。

マッキントッシュが、空間すべてのものをデザインし、一体的な美的調和の世界感を表現したように、建築の強い固有性と世界観は、建築の可能性を拓くと思えるのである。

Hiroaki Kimura is an architect and professor emeritus at Kyoto Institute of Technology. Currently, he is the principle at Hiroaki Kimura+Ks Architects & Associates. From 1978 to 1982, he studied at the Mackintosh School of Architecture at the Glasgow School of Art, and then at the University of Glasgow, where he received his doctoral degree in Mackintosh Studies. He was made an honorary fellow of the Royal Incorporation of Architects in Scotland in 2015 and received an honorary doctorate from the Royal Thai University of Chiang Mai in 2019.

木村博昭は建築家および京都工芸繊維大学名誉教授。現在は Hiroaki Kimura+Ks Architects & Associatesを主宰。1978から1982年にかけてグラスゴー美術学校のマッキントッシュ・スクール・オブ・アーキテクチュアおよびグラスゴー大学で学び、マッキントッシュ研究でグラスゴー大学より博士号を取得。2015年にスコットランド王立建築家協会上級名誉会員となり、2019にはタイ王立チェンマイ大学名誉博士号を授与。

The Life of Charles Rennie Mackintosh

Charles Rennie Mackintosh was born in Glasgow, Scotland, in 1868, the fourth of 11 children and second son of a police officer. From the age of 16, he aspired to be an architect. He studied with the Glasgow architect John Hutchinson under a 5-year apprenticeship, a mandatory part of architectural education at the time, while also attending evening classes at Glasgow School of Art. While engaged in architectural practice during the day, Mackintosh studied basic arts at night. After completing his apprenticeship, he joined the soon-to-be-established firm of John Honeyman and Keppie as a draftsman. In 1902 he became a partner in the firm and remained there until 1913, balancing his personal architectural activities with the institutional practice of the firm. After 1914, he moved to London.

Mackintosh was a versatile all-around architect, based in Glasgow while working in architecture, interiors, furniture, light fixtures, and as a textile designer and artist, like a Renaissance artist. He is known as an important pioneer of art nouveau and art deco during the formative years of modernism, exerting an immeasurable influence on subsequent modernist architects.

In the architectural world of the late 19th century, where traditional trends made up the mainstream, Mackintosh and his colleagues from Glasgow School, through actual creative practice, gradually extended the scope of their practice to simple forms based on a white palette with an emphasis on functionality – premised on a vision of the mechanical civilization to come – and constructed the philosophy and ideals of modernism.

Mackintosh worked in architecture and actively practiced as an architect for fewer than 30 years, from 1890 to 1920, excluding his time at Glasgow School of Art. His design style, however, underwent a series of repeated shifts over a short period, as Mackintosh was an architect who sought to not only respond to the social demands associated with the technological innovations of the time, but to also articulate a sense of the changing times themselves. His early years in the early 1890s began with his mastery of the classical style through an academic architectural education based on the beaux arts model, before he turned toward Arts and Crafts, the avant-garde design movement in England. Influenced by this movement, he then progressed to an art nouveau style of pale colors that make the most of the stretched curves and stained colors that became a Mackintosh trademark.

From 1898 onward, he distinguished himself from the Arts and Crafts movement by developing more geometric, abstract forms based on squares, painting his materials white, pink, black, and silver, and developing a post–art nouveau style. Together with James Herbert MacNair and sisters Margaret and Frances Macdonald, all of them students at the Glasgow School of Art, they formed a design group called The Glasgow Four and developed the original Glasgow style that swiftly became the avant-garde of Europe. He married Margaret Macdonald in 1900.

Their participation in various modern interior design exhibitions in major cities on the continent, such as Berlin, Dresden, Moscow, Paris, Turin, and Vienna showed that Mackintosh and The Glasgow Four had already established an international reputation and significant presence on the continent. One can well imagine the novel stimulation and lasting impact of their work on the architects and artists of the next generation, and certainly they were exactly the kinds of architects-cum-artists that the times demanded.

Mackintosh's later work from 1910 onward made use of strong colors, such as black, and primary colors yellow and blue, before moving into the art deco style of his late career, with more complex geometric forms such as triangles and steps, and a similarly functional and more abstract direction, with a shift toward an international style.

This sort of design transition was also seen in the work of Peter Behrens, Josef Hoffmann, and Joseph Maria Olbrich, architects of the same generation as Mackintosh who likewise began their architectural education in academia, before moving on to art nouveau and art deco. Late 19th-century architects also made this design transition, albeit with something of a time lag.

During his later years, Mackintosh left Glasgow and moved to London, where he began working in his studio. While he was involved in several architectural and textile design projects, no particularly distinguished projects survive, except for the art deco masterpiece Bassett-Lowke house at 78 Derngate (1917–1920, pp. 110–115) and The Dug-Out (1917, pp. 102–103), which was added to the basement of Willow Tea Rooms (pp. 92–103). Contrary to the successes of the Vienna Secession, who were later succeeded by the Bauhaus, Mackintosh left architecture altogether after 1923 and devoted himself to watercolor painting in the south of France. Following a tongue cancer diagnosis, however, he returned to London for treatment in 1925 and died there on December 10, 1928.

Translated by Darryl Jingwen Wee

This page, left: Mackintosh and his friends from Glasgow School of Art. This page, right: Francis Newbery. Photos courtesy of T. & R. Annan and Sons. Opposite: Textile and poster designed by Mackintosh.

本頁、左：マッキントッシュとグラスゴー美術学校の友人たち。本頁、右：フランシス・ニューベリー。右頁：マッキントッシュによるテキスタイル、ポスターのデザイン。

C.R.マッキントッシュの生涯

マッキントッシュは、警察官の11人兄妹の4番目、次男として1868年グラスゴーに生まれ、16歳から建築家を目指す。当時の建築家教育の義務であった5年間のアペアランシップをグラスゴーの建築家ジョン・ハチソンのもとで行い、同時にグラスゴー美術学校の夜間部に入学。日中は建築実務に携わりながら、夜間は基礎芸術を学んでいた。その後、5年間のアペアランシップ終了後、設立間近のジョン・ハニマン・アンド・ケペ事務所にドラフターとして移籍する。その後1902年にパートナーに加わり、1913年まで在籍、個人としての建築家活動と事務所の組織的実務を両立させていた。そして1914年ロンドンに移り住む。

マッキントッシュはルネッサンスの芸術家のように、建築・インテリア・家具・照明器具・テキスタイルと多才でオールラウンドな建築家として、グラスゴーを拠点に活躍していた。彼はモダニズムの形成期であるアール・ヌーヴォー、アール・デコにおいて重要な先駆的役割を果たした人物として知られ、その後のモダニズムを担う建築家達に及ぼした影響は計り知れない。

伝統的風潮が一般的であった19世紀末の建築界にあって、グラスゴー派のマッキントッシュらは、創作活動の実践を通して、機械文明の予感に立脚した、機能性を重視し白を基調としたシンプルな造形へと展開を拡げ、モダニズム理念を構築していく。

マッキントッシュが実務に携わり、建築家として設計活動を行ったのは、グラスゴー美術学校在籍期間を除けば、1890〜1920年頃までの30年足らずの間である。しかしその作風は、短期間のうちに変遷を繰り返した。恐らくマッキントッシュが、当時の技術革新にともなう社会的要求に対応していた建築家であり、変わり行く時代の表現者そのものであったからだと想像できる。1890年代前半はボザールを規範とした建築教育による古典様式の習得に始まり、イングランドの前衛的デザイン運動であるアーツ・アンド・クラフツに傾倒、その影響を受けながらも、マッキントッシュ特有の引き伸ばされたような曲線とステン色などの素材感を生かした淡い色彩を示すアール・ヌーヴォー様式へと進む。1898年以降は、アーツ・アンド・クラフツと一線を画し、正方形を基本とする、より幾何学的抽象形態と、素材を白・ピンク・黒・シルバーに塗り消した、ポスト・アール・ヌーヴォーへと展開。グラスゴー美術学校の仲間であった、ハーバート・マクネイアー、マーガレットとフランシスのマクドナルド姉妹とザ・フォーと呼ばれたデザイナー・グループを組織し、独創的なグラスゴー・スタイルを打ちだし、一躍欧州でアヴァンギャルドとして活躍する。

大陸の主要都市、ウィーン、ドレスデン、ベルリン、トリノ、パリ、モスクワなどで開催された各種のモダン・インテリア・エキシビジョンへの参加は、マッキントッシュおよびザ・フォーの存在が、既にインターナショナルな名声と共に、大陸での重要な立場にあった証であろう。次世代を担う若き建築家、芸術家たちに新鮮な刺激と強いインパクトを与えただろうし、時代が求めていた建築家そのものであったと想像できる。

その後1910年以降のマッキントッシュは、強い色彩の黒・黄・青などの原色を使用し、そして、三角形やステップなどのより複雑な幾何学的形態が織り成すアール・デコ様式と至っている。そして機能性を重視しより抽象的なインターナショナル・スタイルを見通したものに至る。

このようなデザイン変遷は、同世代の建築家であった、ペーター・ベーレンスや、ヨゼフ・ホフマン、ヨゼフ・マリア・オルブリッヒ等、同様にアカデミックな建築教育に始まり、アール・ヌーヴォーからアール・デコに至り、時間差があるにしても、世紀末の建築家が辿ったデザイン変遷でもあったと言えるだろう。

晩年は、グラスゴーを去り、ロンドンに移居しアトリエ活動を始め、いくつかの建築プロジェクトやテキスタイル・デザインを手掛けていたが、アール・デコの秀作となる78ダンゲート（1917〜1920、110〜115頁）およびウィロー・ティー・ルーム（92〜103頁）の地下に増設されたダグアウト・ルーム（1917、102〜103頁）を除けば際立った実作品は残っていない。後のバウハウスに受け継がれる、ウィーン分離派の活躍に反し、1923年以後マッキントッシュはまったく建築の仕事から離れ、南フランスで水彩画に専念していた。しかし舌癌に侵され、1925年にロンドンに戻り治療を受けるが、1928年12月10日にその生涯を終える。

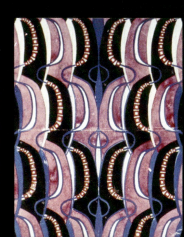

住宅

The Hill House
Helensburgh, United Kingdom 1902–1904

ヒル・ハウス
英国、ヘレンズバラ　1902〜1904

The Beginning of the 20th-Century Modern House
One of Charles Rennie Mackintosh's best-known buildings, The Hill House is considered a masterpiece of early 20th-century modern housing.

Helensburgh, where this house stands, was at the time a new upscale residential area for the middle class. Less than an hour by train from the city of Glasgow, about 20 miles away, Helensburgh also had the industrialization of a developing railroad network and the steam engine. The property sits on top of a small hill overlooking the beautiful landscape of the Clyde Estuary, offering views of the Scottish countryside with its rolling hills. Walter W. Blackie, the client, was an entrepreneur in the Glasgow publishing business; he resided at The Hill House for the next half century until the end of his life.

The Hill House is associated with 2 important and outstanding houses that were also being designed around this time. The first is Windy Hill (1899–1901, pp. 58–65), the first private residence that Mackintosh built and furnished. Like Windy Hill, the plan for The Hill House divides the living and service areas into an L shape at 90 degrees, with rooms and openings designed according to necessity and size, with a greatest emphasis placed on functionality. Based on the vernacular Scottish baronial style, but with a heightened sense of geometric abstraction characteristic of Mackintosh, the design clearly articulates the philosophy of modernism. The other project is House for an Art Lover (1901, pp. 66–71), which Mackintosh designed for a competition based on the theme of a residence for the new century. Like in House for an Art Lover designed as a space for experiencing art in all its forms, a piano in the drawing room alcove of The Hill House connects to the music room, while the drawing room space, enclosed in a brilliant fashion, abounds with abstract stenciled rose motifs and square patterns. The connection between the roses on the walls and the floor lamp shades embroidered with rose motifs, as well as the rose motifs on the stained-glass light fixtures, project a sense of continuity in the space through an integrated ornamental scheme, while everything – the space, furniture, and objects – is carefully controlled. A perfectly realized modern house, The Hill House is a practical attempt to realize the early 20th century modernist philosophy of continuity from the doorknob to the architecture, an ideal that allows for both functionality and artistry.

While Mackintosh designed many of the furnishings for each room in The Hill House, the interior of the dining room was the only space that Blackie wanted to match the Victorian carpet and dining set that had been used by the family for generations, without clashing with it. The result is a testament to Mackintosh's competence and adaptability.

pp. 15, 42 translated by Darryl Jingwen Wee

p. 13: Southwest elevation. Photos on pp. 14, 18–21, 23, 34–37, 40–43, 49 courtesy of Hiroaki Kimura. pp. 14–15: Perspective view toward northeast (1903). Drawing courtesy of Glasgow School of Art. This page: Perspective view toward northwest (1903). Drawings on pp. 16–17 courtesy of The National Trust for Scotland. Opposite: Perspective view toward southeast (1903).

13頁：南西立面。14〜15頁：北東向パースペクティヴ（1903）。本頁：北西向パースペクティヴ（1903）。右頁：南東向パースペクティヴ（1903）。

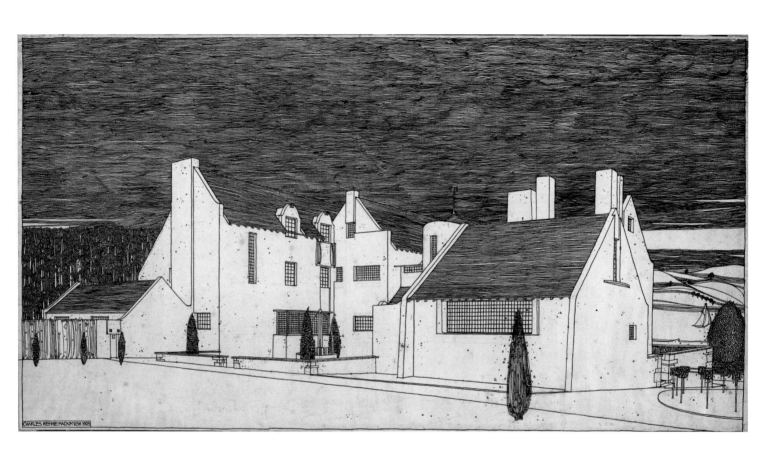

20世紀のモダン住宅の始まり

ヒル・ハウスは、マッキントッシュの代表作であり、20世紀初頭のモダン住宅の秀作とされ、その名を歴史上に残した作品である。
この住宅の建つヘレンズバラは、中産階級達のために開発された新興の高級住宅地であり、蒸気機関の発達と共に鉄道網が整備され、グラスゴー市内から20マイル離れた汽車で1時間足らずの所にある。自然の広がるクライド河口の美しい景色を望む小高い丘の上に建ち、丘の連なるスコットランドの田園風景が見下ろせる敷地である。クライアントは、グラスゴーで出版業を営む実業家、ウォルター・W・ブラッキー氏であった。ブラッキーは人生を終えるまでの半世紀間、このヒル・ハウスに住まう。

ヒル・ハウスの背景には、同時期にデザインされていた重要な秀作となる2つの住宅がある。一つ目は、マッキントッシュがはじめて建築から家具までを手掛けた個人住宅、ウィンディー・ヒル（1899〜1901、58〜65頁）である。プランはウィンディー・ヒルと同様に、居住部とサービス部を90度のL型に分節し、部屋の広さや開口部等は、その必要性と大きさに応じ、より機能性に重点を置くデザインである。そして、バナキュラーなスコティッシュ・バロニアル様式をもとに、マッキントッシュ特有の幾何学的抽象性をより高め、モダニズムへの理念を明確に表現している。もう一つは、新世紀の住まいをテーマとしたコンペ案として応募した、芸術愛好家の家（1901、66〜71頁）である。ここで構想されたのは、総合的芸術の体験空間としての住宅で、居間のアルコーヴにピアノを置き、ミュージック・ルームと結びつけ、更に、花々に囲われた居室空間は、抽象化されたステンシル画の薔薇のモチーフと正方形模様で埋め尽くされ、壁面の薔薇と薔薇モチーフを刺繍したスタンド・シェードとの繋がり、薔薇モチーフが施されたステンドガラスの照明器具など、一体装飾による空間の連続性を示し、空間と家具およびオブジェ類に至るすべてがコントロールされた住まいである。

20世紀初頭に、モダニズムの理念であるドアノブから建築に至る連続性を成す、機能性と芸術性が両立する理想を実践的に試みた、完成度の高いモダン住宅である。

マッキントッシュは、このヒル・ハウスで多くの家具を各部屋に合わせデザインしているが、ダイニング空間は、唯一ブラッキーの希望であった、一族が歴代使用していたヴィクトリア朝のカーペットとダイニングセットに合わせ、違和感のない空間に仕上げられ、マッキントッシュの力量と順応性を示している。

pp. 18–19: Southwest elevation. p. 20: North exterior of staircase. p. 21: Approach to the main entrance. Opposite: Southwest elevation. Photo by Shinkenchiku-sha. This page, top: South grass lawn. The Glyde River and hills in the distance are visible from main entrance. This page, bottom left: Backdoor to the south lawn. This page, bottom right: Front gate.

18〜19頁：南西立面。20頁：北側の階段室外観。21頁：正面玄関へのアプローチ。左頁：南西立面。本頁、上：芝の広がる南庭。傾斜する円弧状のアプローチから正面玄関へ向うと、グライド川と丘陵が連なるランドスケープが眼下に広がる。本頁、左下：南庭の勝手口。本頁、右下：正面門。

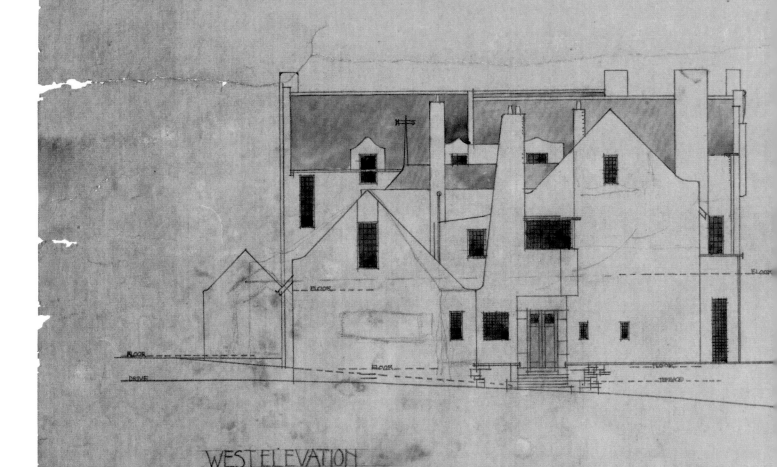

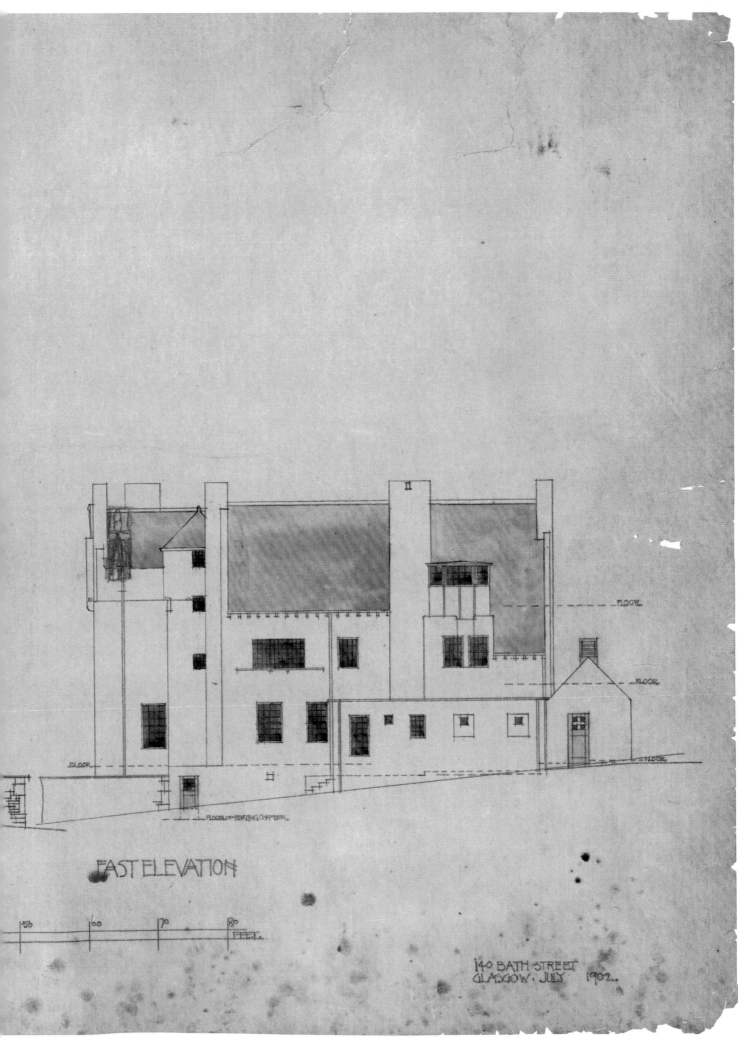

HOUSE AT HELENSBURGH
FOR W.W. BLACKIE ESQ.

PLAN OF GROUND FLOOR.

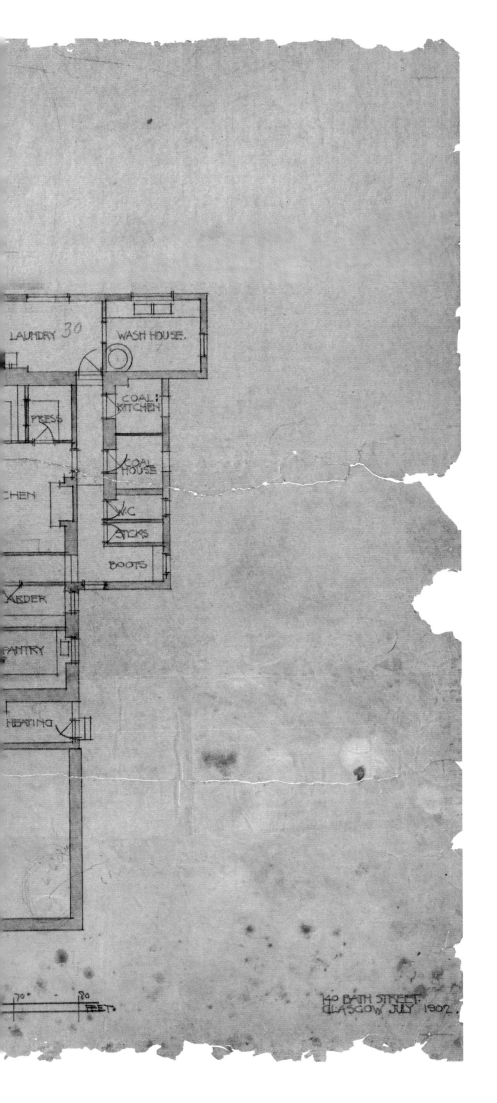

pp. 24–25: West (left) and east (right) elevations (July 1902, original scale: 1/96). Drawings on pp. 24–29 courtesy of Strathclyde University Archives. This page: Ground floor plan (July 1902, original scale: 1/96). Main rooms are located south of the L-shaped plan, while services, such as kitchen, are in the east. The billiard room, next to the stairs in Mackintosh's proposal, was never built. A wall on the east side of the drawing room was removed to create an alcove where a piano is placed.

24～25頁：西立面図（左）、東立面図（右）（1902年7月、原図縮尺：1/96）。本頁：地上階平面図（1902年7月、原図縮尺：1/96）。L型平面の構成、南ブロックに主室、東ブロックには、キッチン等サーヴィス部が配置される。実現案では階段横のビリヤード・ルームは建設されていない。また居間の東側の小部屋の壁がなくなり、できたアルコーヴにピアノが置かれている。

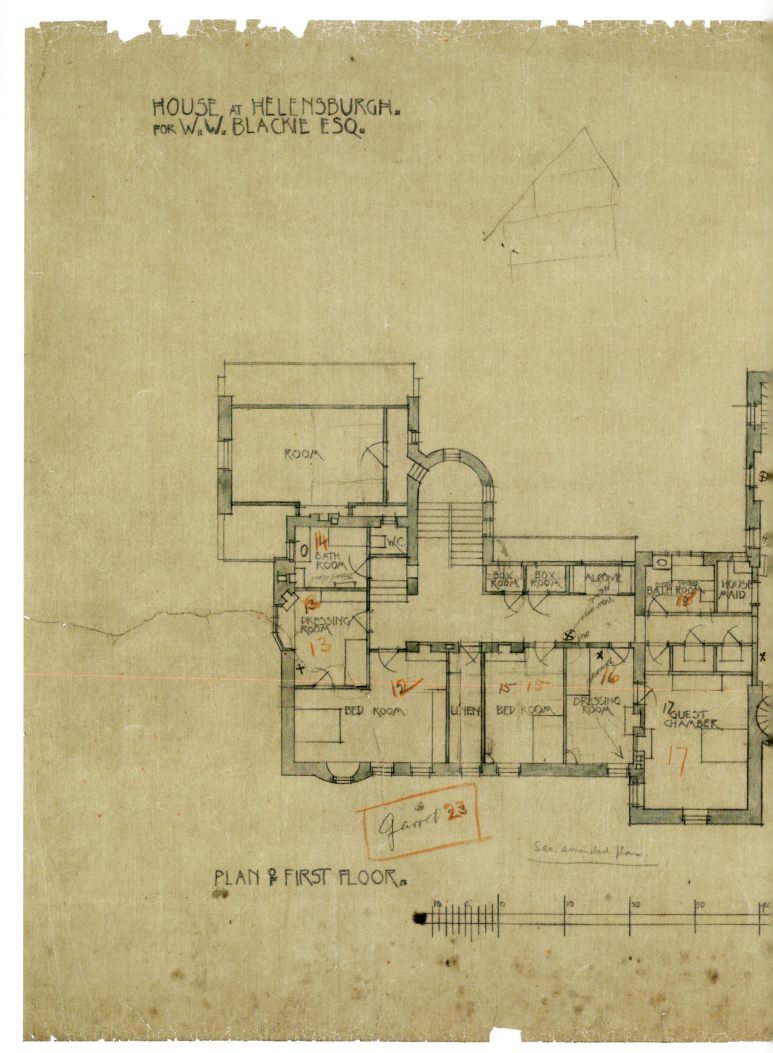

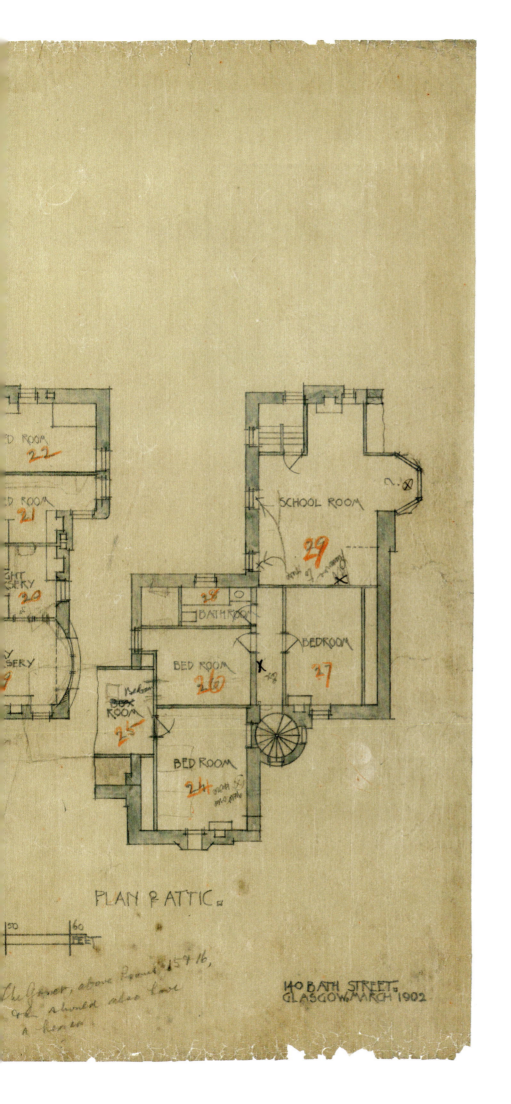

This page: Second-floor (left) and attic-floor (right) plans (March 1902, original scale: 1/96). The master bedroom and guest room are located south of the second floor, while childrens' rooms are located east of attic.

本頁:2階平面図(左)、屋根裏階平面図(右) (1902年3月、原図縮尺:1/96)。2階には南に主寝室・客室が、東側の屋根裏階には子供部屋が配される。

p. 30: View of the hall from the entrance. Photos on pp. 30–33, 38–39, 46–48 by Johan Dehlin, courtesy of Carmody Groarke. p. 31: The hall has dark and heavy appearance in contrast to the white exterior and main room. Rugs, furniture, and light fixtures consistently incorporate a square motif. pp. 32–33: View of the main entrance from the hall, with the stairs visible on the right. pp. 34–35: Sunroom, south of the drawing room. This page: The mosaic mantelpiece of the drawing room.

30頁：玄関からホールを見る。31頁：ホールでは白い外観と主室とは対照的な黒く重厚な様相を示す。敷物・家具・照明器具などに一貫して正方形の装飾がデザインされた。32〜33頁：ホールから正面玄関を奥に、階段を右に見る。34〜35頁：居間、南のサンルームを見る。本頁：モザイク装飾のなされた居間のマントルピース。

This page, top: The library is located immediately to the right of the main entrance. This page, bottom: Dining room. The room was designed to match furnishings (table, chairs, shelves, and carpet) originally owned by the Blackie family. Opposite: Staircase.

本頁、上：書斎、正面玄関を入ってすぐ右に位置する。本頁、下：ダイニング・ルーム。クライアントのブラッキー家が元々所有していた調度品（テーブル、椅子、棚、カーペット）に合わせた空間。右頁：階段室。

Interior of the Second-Floor Bedroom: Architect as Total Designer

The design motifs in Mackintosh's watercolors are the nature and slender female forms found in art nouveau. Similarly, Mackintosh's spatial images are spaces suited to these slender figures, with plants everywhere and surrounded by Mackintosh's trademark rose motifs. There is no image of masculinity in its spatial context.

While Mackintosh is often seen as more interior furniture designer than architect, his approach to design clearly reflects the exigencies of the architectural concept, such as use and function. For example, the main bedroom on the second floor consists of a living area and bed space, with large windows on the living side, a fireplace at the far end of the side with the entrance to the room, and a sofa in a niche next to a recessed bookshelf, with a light above them. The bed space has a cavernous vaulted ceiling, and is delicately designed with a small window and an inner door to block out the light. There is also a standing full-length mirror on the window side, at the same height as the window opening. With light coming in from both sides, one's reflection can be seen in the mirror. A light fixture is also installed above the mirror. Functionality and necessity determine everything. In the detailed elevation plan for the bedroom, the furniture and the space are drawn together, the scale of the furniture matches the height and length of the windows, and the decorative pattern of the stenciled roses on the wall and the curtains are all conceived as part of a single, integrated space, with the design of the space, built-in moldings, furniture, and curtains all given equal weight in a single drawing. The high-backed Ladder Back Chair, The Hill House's most outstanding feature, goes beyond the simple function of a chair; it also takes on an object-like symbolism in the bedroom. Placed between 2 wardrobes, it can be used as a seat, but also a place for small items and bags, while the high back can be used to hang clothes as well. The height of this high-backed chair is the same as that of the niche sofa, and the ladder back latticework creates a continuous relationship with the stenciled patterns on the wall that projects a 3-dimensional effect around it, as if the roses twined around a hedge. In this way, the rose hedges planted in the garden form a connection and continuity between the inside and outside. This ideal house, in which every detail of the space has been carefully considered by Mackintosh, seeks to realize both a lived reality and an artistic, aesthetic harmony.

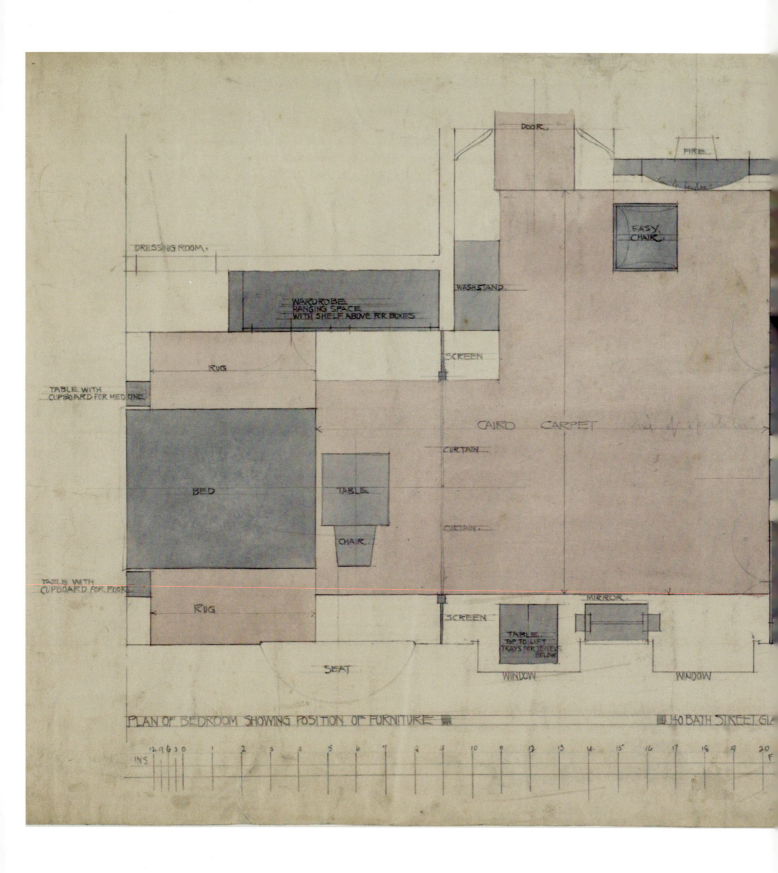

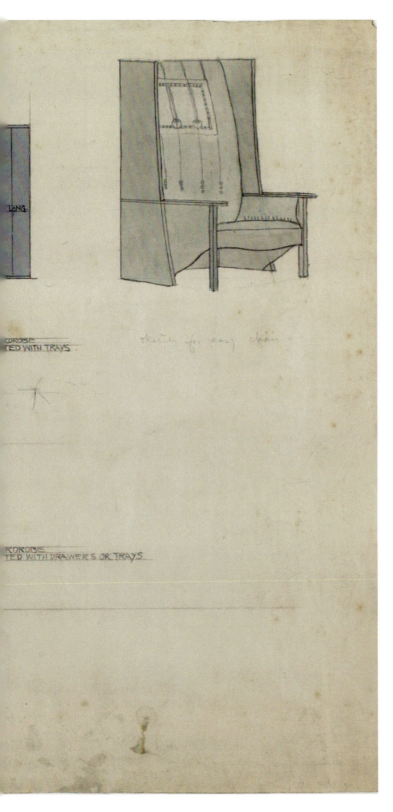

2階寝室のインテリア：トータル・デザイナーの建築家

マッキントッシュの水彩画のデザイン・モチーフは、アール・ヌーヴォーに登場する、自然と細身の人物像である。同様に、マッキントッシュの空間イメージは、細身の身体が似合う空間であり、いたるところに植物があり、マッキントッシュのシンボルである薔薇モチーフで囲まれている。男性的な空間イメージは感じない。

マッキントッシュは、しばしば、建築家というより、インテリア家具デザイナーとしてとらえられるが、そのデザインの手法は建築的考え方にもとづき、用途や機能、必要性により決定されている。たとえば、2階の主寝室は、居間的スペースとベッド・スペースで構成され、居間側には大きな窓をとり、部屋の入り口側の奥に暖炉、そして本棚の窪みとその横には、こもれる様なニッチのソファーがあり、その上部には照明がある。ベッド・スペースは、洞穴のようなヴォールト天井であり、小さな窓と光を遮蔽できるように内扉を設けた繊細なデザインが行なわれている。また、窓際には、姿見のスタンド家具があり、高さは、窓の開口に合わせ、両サイドから光が入り、鏡に自分が映しだされ、その姿見の上部にも照明がある。すべては、機能性と必要性で決定されている。ベッドルームの詳細展開図には、家具と空間が一緒に描かれ、家具のスケールは窓の高さや長押に合わせられ、壁面ステンシルの薔薇の装飾模様やカーテンも、すべては一体として空間構想がなされ、空間、造付け造作、家具からカーテンのデザインに至るまで一枚の図面上に等分に描かれている。そして、ヒル・ハウスの中で最秀作となるハイバックのラダーバック・チェアは、単なる椅子の機能を超え、寝室においてオブジェのような象徴性を兼ね備え、ワードローブ間に置かれている。座面には座る事も出来るが小物やバックを置け、ハイバックの背板は服を掛ける機能性をもつ。そしてハイバックの高さは、ニッチソファーの背高と同じに合わせられ、ラダーバックの格子は、壁面に描かれたステンシル模様と合わさって、垣根に薔薇が絡まったような前後の立体感のある連続的な関係性を生じさせる。こうして、庭園に植えられた薔薇の垣根群と、内と外が連続するのである。ヒル・ハウスは空間の隅々まで熟考され、住まうリアリティと芸術的な美的調和をマッキントッシュが追求した理想の住宅である。

pp. 40–41: Master bedroom. The room is divided into a living area and bed space. pp. 42–43: Bed space with cavernous vaulted ceiling. This page: Detailed floor plan of master bedroom (circa 1903, original scale: 1/24). Drawing courtesy of The Hunterian, University of Glasgow.

40〜41頁：主寝室。部屋内で居間エリアとベッド・エリアに分節される。42〜43頁：ヴォールト天井のベッド・エリア。本頁：主寝室平面詳細図（1903年頃、原図縮尺：1/24）。

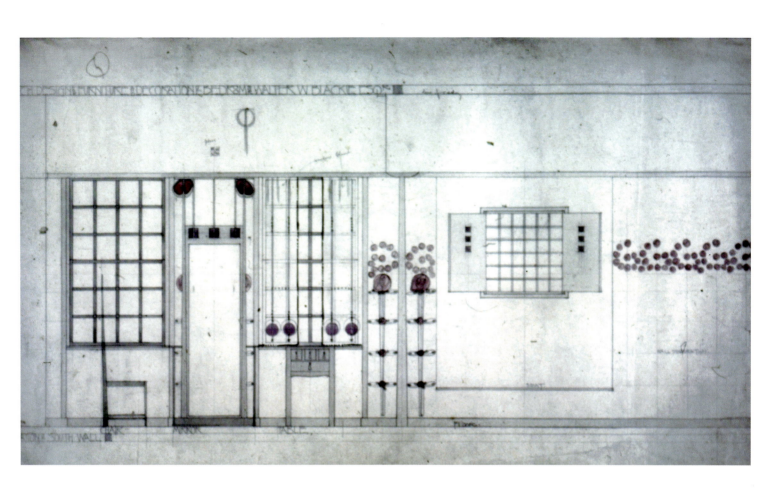

pp. 46–47: Windows facing south. Capitalizing on the natural lighting, a full length mirror is placed between the windows with a light fixture above. Rose motifs are designed to match the furniture, light fixtures, and opening height and muntins of the windows. Opposite: Ladder Back Chair is placed between built-in closets with a sofa in the adjacent niche. This page, top: Master bedroom elevation (circa 1903, original scale: 1/24). This page, bottom left: Master bedroom entrance, fireplace, and built-in sofa. This page, bottom right: A small window with shutters next to the bed.

46〜47頁：南向きの窓。採光を考慮し姿見が窓の間に置かれ、上部には吊り照明がある。薔薇模様の壁面ステンシルが、家具・吊りの照明・開口の高さや窓サッシュのグリッドに合わせて描かれている。左頁：造付け収納の間にラダーバック・チェアが置かれ、その隣のニッチにはソファが設られた。本頁、上：主寝室展開図（1903年頃、原図縮尺：1/24）。本頁、左下：主寝室入口、暖炉と造付けソファを見る。本頁、下：ベッドに面した内扉のある小窓。

Essay:
A Temporary House for a House
Andy Groarke

エッセイ：
住宅のための仮設住宅
アンディ・グローク
土居純訳

The Hill House (pp. 12–49) is one of Charles Rennie Mackintosh's most significant works, one of Scotland's most acclaimed buildings, and a seminal example of early 20th-century European architecture. Built in 1902 for the publisher Walter Blackie and his young family, it is situated in Helensburgh, 30 km west of Glasgow, and commands panoramic views over River Clyde Estuary.

My first visit to The Hill House was during my first year of architecture school in 1990, as part of a class field trip to study Glasgow's architecture. A visit to the house was then part of a well-trodden pilgrimage to most of Mackintosh's limited, but fairly well-preserved built work in and around Glasgow. While I was familiar with Mackintosh's beguiling perspective drawings of the house, and perhaps conscious of some of its published interior photography, experiencing the house in person made a profound impression. I recall the stark composition of weighty forms in grayish rendering, and its emphatic presence within the exposure of the Scottish landscape and unyielding weather. In contrast to its context, this architecture demonstrated a defiant presence and appeared to be designed and built to last forever. My next visit to The Hill House would be more than a quarter century later, as part of an organized tour for architects who would compete to build a small, temporary visitors' center beside this world-renowned house, a contest that later evolved into a bolder vision to meet the challenges of keeping The Hill House alive while essential and overdue repairs are undertaken.

Mackintosh's domestic masterpiece sits like a 20th-century Scottish tower house, with its roughcast walls, picturesque slate roofline, asymmetrical disposition of windows, and absence of historical ornament. The house proposed a radical layout and 3-dimensional spatial progression, and although the architecture was embedded in the tradition of Scottish baronial, Mackintosh was also clearly influenced by the contemporary technological advances of modernism happening elsewhere in Europe. This construction of the building has led to some fundamental long-term problems of prolonged water damage. The concrete rendering Mackintosh used to smother the entire building and unite the composition of eclectic forms in one coherent (and now iconic) image is not as forgiving as the vernacular solution of lime-based roughcast rendering; concrete rendering cracks in the freezing cold and lets water in, but it doesn't let water out.

For nearly 120 years many have tried to solve the water ingress problem, and all have failed. Various patches of the concrete rendering that Mackintosh chose to use, especially around wall heads and chimneys, have been applied in a vain

ヒル・ハウス（12〜49頁）は、チャールズ・レニー・マッキントッシュの代表作に数えられ、また欧州建築が黄金期にあった20世紀初頭に建てられたスコットランド屈指の名作である。1902年に出版業者ウォルター・ブラッキーのために建てられたこの住宅は、グラスゴーから西に30km離れたヘレンズバラにあり、クライド河口を一望のもとに見渡す。

私がはじめてヒル・ハウスを訪れたのは、大学一年生だった1990年のことである。その年の研修旅行がグラスゴー建築巡りだったのだ。ヒル・ハウスは当時、グラスゴー周辺でも数少ない比較的保存状態のよい実作で、マッキントッシュ詣での定番の目的地であった。この住宅については、マッキントッシュ自筆の魅力的なパース画やあの有名な内観写真もあったためすっかり見知った気でいたが、ところが実際に訪れてみるとやはり感慨もひとしおだった。今でもありありと目に浮かぶ。グレーがかった壁の重厚なフォルムを組み合わせたその力強い構成、そしてスコットランドの風景と過酷な気候の中に凛として佇むあの存在感が。そんな背景からくっきりと浮き上がった姿は、あたかも不朽の建築として設計され建てられたかに見えた。二度目の訪問の機会は、四半世紀あまり経って訪れた。この世界的名住宅の脇に小さなヴィジター・センターを仮設することになり、その設計コンペの参加建築家を集めて現地視察が企画されたのだった。そしてこのコンペから、なんとも大胆な構想が導きだされた。ヒル・ハウスを閉鎖せずに、喫緊の課題であった大規模修繕を行なうというものだ

マッキントッシュの名作住宅は、さしずめ20世紀に現れたスコットランド式の城館である。外壁はラフキャスト（掃付け）仕上げ、スレート屋根はピクチャレスクな輪郭を描き、窓割りは非対称、歴史的装飾は皆無である。家の間取りは斬新で、経路は三次元に展開する。建築としてはスコティッシュ・バロニアル様式の系譜にありながら、明らかに同時代の欧州、ことに最新技術を用いたモダニズムの影響が認められる。この工法ゆえに、雨水の浸潤という大問題がつきまとうことになる。マッキントッシュは外壁全体にポルトランド・セメントを塗り込めることで、種々のフォルムを折衷するようにして全体を構成し、（いまやアイコニックな）イメージをまとめ上げた。だがこの工法は、在来の石灰ベースのラフキャスト仕上げと比べて遊びが少ない。凍てつく寒さがセメント表面にクラック（ひび割れ）を生じさせ、そこへいったん水が浸入すると二度と抜けることはない。

この120年近くの間に、大勢の人間がこの浸潤問題を解決しようと試みたが、いずれも失敗に終わった。マッキントッシュが当初用いたセメントをそのイメージどおりに復古させるべく、特に壁上端や煙突まわりは幾度も塗り直されたものの、やはり徒労に終わった。修復時には室内壁の漆喰も塗り直されたが、やはり浸潤による傷みは進んだ。なまじ建物に歴史的価値があったばかりに、なまじマッキントッシュの原設計がほぼそのまま残った稀少例であったばかりに、保存修復に携わる専門家と法人組織は座視するばかりで、みすみす建物を風化させた。つい

or nostalgic attempt to keep the image of the original building intact. Internal walls have been restored and replastered, only to be water damaged again. Because of the building's heritage status and its preciousness as the prime example of an almost untouched Mackintosh design, conservation experts and statutory bodies could do nothing and their inaction resulted in further degradation. The deterioration of the fabric eventually became so serious that the fabric of the house was described by its custodians, The National Trust for Scotland, as "dissolving like an aspirin."

The "box" was first and foremost a punctual response to the need for a major conservation project to help the house survive, an urgent push to stop the clock, halt further decay, and buy time to consider the house's future. Rather than incarcerate the house away from view during restoration, a radical approach to active conservation was taken. With the restoration process estimated to take as long as 15 years, the project was placed in a temporary museum on the site to contain and protect The Hill House as an "artifact" while maintaining visitors' access to the house. a large, profiled steel roof covers the central box of the house, 3 m all around and 18 m high at the apex. This approach keeps 90% of the rain away from the deteriorated construction and provides ample working space for conservation work to take place beneath.

The planform of this protective roof respects the terraced landscaping of the sloping site and includes a compact, prefabricated building for a basic visitor center. With a footprint that touches the ground as little as possible around the terraced podium of the house, while its perimeter negotiates the mature landscape of the original garden design, the box retains trees and planting inside and outside of the enclosure. The visitor center sits beside the west-gable entrance of the house. Made of smooth, dark-stained timber, it forms a counterpoint to the gray roughcast of the house's exterior and provides a prelude to the house's broody interior.

The box's lightweight, supporting structure takes its formal and functional language from pylon construction, with an elemental, galvanized steel frame bolted together; welding was not permitted because of fire risk, especially given the immediate context of the second devastating inferno at Mackintosh's Glasgow School of Art (pp. 116–151) in June 2018. The structure was prefabricated and bolted together at a local Glaswegian steelyard. Once on site, the box was carefully craned into place, covering the house and forming the first layer of protective skeletal frame.

The walls cladding the skeleton were made from a thin membrane of stainless-steel chainmail (32.4 million links in total) that creates a unique environment of a "drying room" within the shelter. Glass was briefly considered but it would not have allowed the house to dry passively and would have turned the house into a relic, an inanimate exhibit, set in a giant vitrine. As part of the construction process, the team worked alongside Glaswegian steel fabricators throughout assembly, teaching them to delicately sew together individual sheets of chainmail that now cover the structure. Wind can breeze through the veil of links, but driving rain quickly loses momentum and does not reach the house. In counterpart to the load-bearing permanence of The Hill House's architecture, the chainmail also allows the box to appear both provisional and transparent; while preventing birds from entering its enclosure, it allows bees to pass through the surface to pollinate the garden landscape within. Through the design of bespoke joints and connections, the structure can be deconstructed and reused once conservation work of the house is complete, saving a significant amount of energy used to fabricate the steel structure.

Carried by the skeletal steel frame, a network of elevated walkways and staircases encourage visitors to promenade up and over the house, enabling previously unseen views of it and its landscape setting. Within this protective, ethereal enclosure and abstracted from its context and environment, The Hill House has an uncanny, objective quality rather like a distressed architectural model or even a well-used doll's house. From these new vantage points, visitors can have a roofer's-eye perspective and ponder for themselves the effect 12 decades of unremitting deterioration have had on the image of Mackintosh's residential masterpiece.

The intention of the big box is not only to serve the pragmatic requirements of a temporary construction shelter, but also to underscore that conservation of The Hill House is more than tackling a physical problem and more than an endeavor related to aesthetic nostalgia; it is also a philosophical pursuit – the careful consideration of how and why we should conserve our built heritage, and how we involve people in that debate.

に管理側のスコットランド・ナショナル・トラストが「水に溶けゆくアスピリン錠」と形容するまでに建物の傷みは進行した。

この住宅を延命させるには大がかりな保存プロジェクトを実施するほかなく、したがってこの「箱」はあくまでそれに向けての応急措置である。これ以上腐食が進まぬよう、まずは時計の針を止めて時間稼ぎをしている合間に今後の手立てを検討する必要があった。ただし修復工事中も住宅を覆い隠さず、反対に保存の過程を積極的に見せることにした。15年がかりともいわれる修復工事の一環として敷地内に仮設ミュージアムを建て、そこにヒル・ハウスを「展示品」として収め、その間も住宅内部を見学できるようにする。「箱」には家型のスティール製大屋根を架けた。この屋根はヒル・ハウスの外側に3mずつ張り出し、最大高さは地上18mに達する。これだけでも傷んだ壁に当たる雨量は90％減り、かつ作業スペースを十分に確保できる。

傾斜地を活かした庭の段に合わせて大屋根の平面形態を決め、その屋根の下に小さなプレファブ棟を置いてヴィジター・センターに充てた。箱の接地面積を極力抑えるようにしてヒル・ハウスの基壇を囲い込みつつ、その外周が、すっかり生い茂った庭の景色と干渉しないよう配置し、足元の草木を保存した。ヴィジター・センターをヒル・ハウスの西の妻入側に置き、その板張りの外壁を濃色かつ平滑に仕上げることで、ヒル・ハウスの淡いグレーのラフキャストの外壁と対比させ、かつ陰影を帯びた住宅内部への導入部を演出した。

箱の軽量構造については、高圧線鉄塔の形態・機能言語を踏襲するかたちで単純な亜鉛めっき鋼のフレームをボルトで接合した。溶接が認められなかったのは、火災の危険があるため、それこそ2018年6月にマッキントッシュ設計のグラスゴー美術学校（116〜151頁）が再び大火災に見舞われたためである。地元グラスゴーの鉄工所で製作されボルト接合された架構を現場に搬入し、これをクレーンでヒル・ハウスに被せるようにして「箱」を組み立て、骨組みの基層とした。

この骨組みにステンレス製リング型ワイヤーメッシュ（総リング数3,240万）を張り、シェルター内を一風変わった「乾燥室」に仕立てた。一時はガラスで覆うことも考えたが、ガラスにするとヒル・ハウスを自然乾燥させられず、しかもそれを過去の遺物として巨大なガラスケースに鎮座させる格好になる。工事中は設計チームが現場に入り、ワイヤーメッシュを一枚一枚丁寧に縫い合わせるようグラスゴーの鉄工業者に細かく指示をだした。風はメッシュの網目を抜けるが、雨はメッシュに当たると勢いを失うので奥の住宅には届かない。ヒル・ハウスがいかにも耐力性にすぐれてびくともしないのとは対照的に、ワイヤーメッシュの箱は透き通って儚げである。このメッシュは鳥の侵入を防ぎつつ、庭の花粉を運んでくる蜂は通す。接合部には特注のジョイントを用いているため、ひとたび保存工事が完了すれば箱の架構を解体し再利用することもできるので、鋼材の製造・組立てにか

かるエネルギーの大幅削減にもなる。

スティール製の骨組みに空中通路と階段とを差し架け、ヒル・ハウスのすぐ上を見学者が回遊できるようにすると、これまで誰も見ることのなかった視点からこの住宅と周囲の風景を眺められる。周囲の文脈や環境から遊離してこの空気のごとく軽い囲いの中に置かれたヒル・ハウスはどこか不気味な物体めいており、むしろたびれた建築模型とか古ぼけた人形の家を思わせる。こうして屋根職人の視点を得た見学者は、120年の歳月をしみじみ感ずることだろう。いかに時の流れがマッキントッシュの名作住宅を劣化させ、その印象を曇らせてきたかを。

単に工事用の仮設シェルターが必要だからこの大箱をつくったのではない。これには人々の意識を喚起する狙いもある。ひとくちにヒル・ハウスを保存するとはいえ、そこには物理的な問題もあれば、往時の美学の問題もあり、さらには哲学的な問題もある。なぜ私たちはこの建物遺産を保存しなければならないのか、どのように保存すべきか、そしてこの議論にどのように人々を巻き込んでゆくか、が問われることになる。

Andy Groarke has over 20 years' experience as an architect, leading the development of award-winning projects including the V&A Members' Room in London, Windermere Jetty Museum in London's Lake District, and The Hill House Box. Groarke began his career working at David Chipperfield Architects in London for 4 years where he met Kevin Carmody. His next 4 years were spent at Hawkins Brown, before establishing Carmody Groarke in 2006. The practice has since developed a reputation for working internationally on a wide range of arts, cultural, heritage, and residential projects, both new build and within the context of historic buildings.

アンディ・グロークは、20年以上の実績をもつ建築家。実作にロンドンのV&Aメンバー・ルーム、湖水地方のウィンダミア・ジェッティ美術館、ヒル・ハウス・ボックスなどがある。ロンドンのデイヴィッド・チッパーフィールド事務所に4年、その後ホーキンス・ブラウンに4年勤務。チッパーフィールド事務所の旧同僚ケヴィン・カーモディとともに2006年にカーモディ・グロークを設立。以来、芸術・文化・遺産・住宅など幅広い分野で新旧のプロジェクトを手がけ、国際的評価を得る。

p. 51: Close-up of stainless-steel chainmail. Photos on pp. 51–57 by Johan Dehlin, courtesy of Carmody Groarke. pp. 54–55: The "box" covering The Hill House. pp. 56–57: Inside the "box."

51頁:ステンレス製リング型ワイヤーメッシュのクロースアップ。54〜55頁:ヒル・ハウス全体を覆う「箱」。56〜57頁:「箱」の内部。

Windy Hill
Kilmacolm, United Kingdom 1899–1901

ウィンディ・ヒル
英国、キルマコーム　1899〜1901

pp. 58–59: Perspective view toward southwest. Drawings on pp. 58–59, 63 courtesy of Glasgow School of Art. This page: East exterior with its large undulating wall and entrance gate. Photos on pp. 60–61 courtesy of Hiroaki Kimura. Opposite: Exterior view toward southwest.

58〜59頁：南西向パースペクティヴ図。本頁：東立面、大きくうねる外壁と玄関ゲートが特徴的。右頁：外観を南西に見る。

Folk House Style Scottish: From Baronial Style to Modernist Design

Windy Hill, like The Hill House (pp. 12–49), stands atop a hill overlooking a beautiful Scottish landscape. Kilmacolm is part of a suburban residential area, southwest of Glasgow, that developed along with the railroad network in the 19th century. This was the first private residence where Charles Rennie Mackintosh cultivated a comprehensive, aesthetically harmonious space, from the landscape exterior to the architecture, interiors, and furniture. It was also a precursor to The Hill House, a modern residence for the 20th century. The client was a lifelong friend of Mackintosh's, businessman William Davidson.

Like Red House and The Hill House, Windy Hill has an L-shaped plan, with the main room along the south side, a back service room on the west side, and bedrooms on the upper floor. At the time, the *mingei* philosophy of the functional beauty of folk houses, as seen in Charles Francis Annesley Voysey, which broke away from the classical architectural style that had been the norm since Greek times, had become a new trend in England along with the Arts and Crafts movement, and Mackintosh was fully aware of this philosophy.

The exterior of Windy Hill with its large undulating stone walls and Mackintosh's sensitive response to it was an early practical experiment in the rustic Scottish baronial style, a folk house style from the Scottish region. Its design features a greater degree of abstraction, highlighting simple, essential openings that feel contemporary even today.

Windy Hill is also a transitional work that blends the pale greenish painted furniture of the Arts and Crafts movement with the clear black and white furniture and white spaces that distinguish Mackintosh's later designs.

Although Mackintosh belonged to the architectural firm Honeyman and Keppie, Davidson may have been a private client of his. The Dean of Guild (D&G) for Windy Hill was signed by Mackintosh himself, not the firm. Presumably, he was officially licensed as an architect at this time. After 1902, he became a partner in the firm as Honeyman, Keppie and Mackintosh.

Translated by Darryl Jingwen Wee

民家様式スコティッシュ：バロニア様式からモダニズム・デザインへ

ウィンディ・ヒルは、ヒル・ハウス（12〜49頁）同様、スコットランドの美しい風景を見下ろす丘の上に建つ。キルマコルムは、グラスゴー郊外の南西部に位置する街で、鉄道網の整備によって開発された郊外住宅地である。マッキントッシュが、ランドスケープの外構から、建築、インテリア、家具に至るまでデザインを総合的な美的調和の空間に仕上げ、20世紀のモダン住宅であるヒル・ハウスの前進となった、最初の個人住宅である。クライアントは、マッキントッシュの生涯の友人であった実業家のウィリアム・デヴィットソンである。

平面は、レッド・ハウス、ヒル・ハウスと同様にL型プランであり、南面に主室となる部屋と西面にバックサービスの部屋を配し、上階に寝室を設け、機能性を重視した提案であった。当時、アーツ・アンド・クラフツと共に、ギリシャの時代から延々とつながる規範と成っていた古典の建築様式から離反した、チャールズ・フランシス・アネスリー・ヴォイジーに見られる民家様式の用美の理念は、英国における新潮流であり、マッキントッシュも十分にその理念を理解していた。

ウィンディ・ヒルの外観は、大きくうねった石塀をもち、マッキントッシュも敏感に反応した、スコットランド地方の民家様式である素朴なスコティッシュ・バロニア様式を、逸早く実践的に試み、より抽象性を高め、現在につながる簡素で必要性に応じた開口など、モダニズムの理念にもとづいたデザインを構築している。

また、アーツ・アンド・クラフツ派の淡いグリーンニッシュに塗られた家具と、その後のマッキントッシュ・デザインの特色である黒白色の明解な家具と白い空間が混じり合う、過渡期の作品である。

マッキントッシュは、当時ハニマン・アンド・ケペ事務所に所属していたが、マッキントッシュの個人的クライアントであったのであろうか、ウィンディヒルのディーン・オブ・ギルド（建築確認提出図面）には建築家として事務所名でなく、マッキントッシュの署名が記録されている。恐らく、この頃に正式に建築家資格を得ていたと思われる。1902年以降、ハニマン・ケペ・アンド・マッキントッシュとして事務所のパートナーになっている。

Opposite, top: North elevation (June 1900, original scale: 1/96). Opposite, bottom: Ground-floor plan (June 1900, original drawing scale: 1/96).

右頁、上：北立面図（1900年6月、原図縮尺：1/96）。右頁、下：地上階平面図（1900年6月、原図縮尺：1/96）。

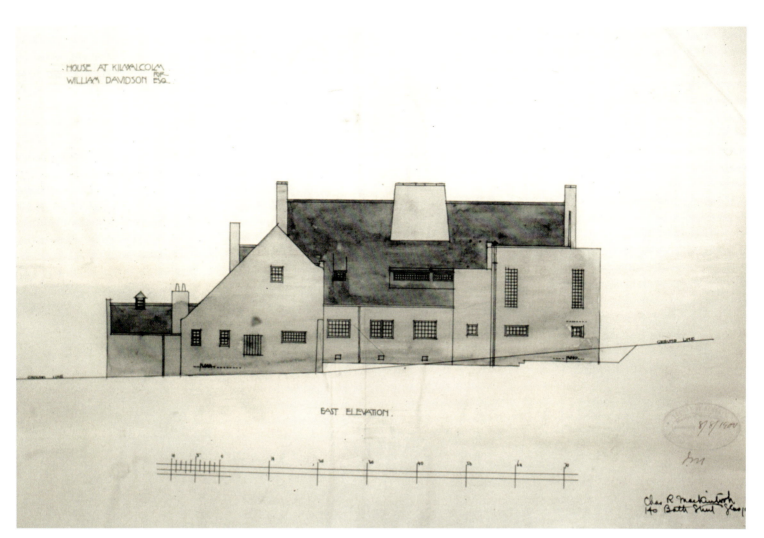
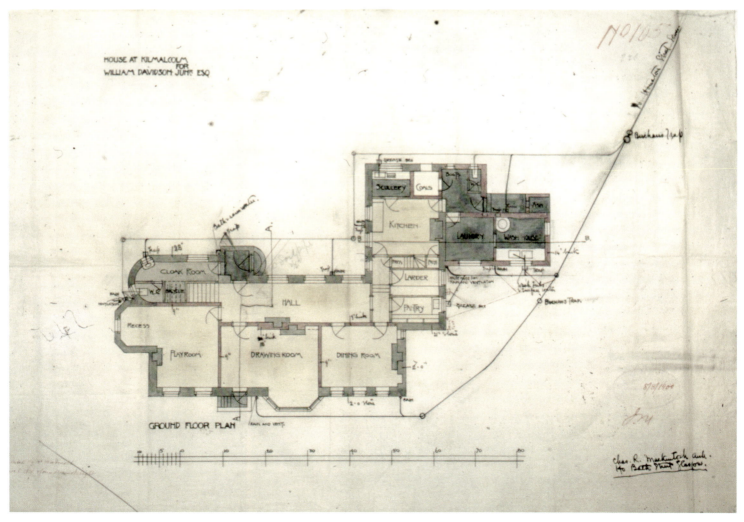

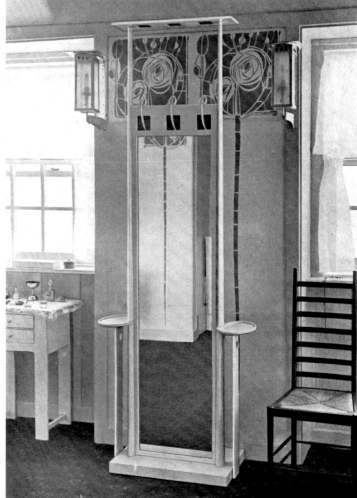

Opposite, top: Sunroom in the drawing room, photo taken circa 1901. Photos on p. 64 courtesy of T. & R. Annan and Sons. Opposite, bottom: Main hall, photo taken circa 1901. This page, top: Drawing room fireplace. Photo from Dekorative Kunst *no. 5, 1902, p. 199. This page, bottom: Master bedroom. A full length mirror is placed between the windows with a pair of bracket lights on either side. A rose motif is stenciled on the back wall, with a middle-backed Ladder Back Chair next to it. The composition of the living room and master bedroom is similar to that of The Hill House. Photo from* Dekorative Kunst *no. 5, 1902, p. 203.*

左頁、上：居間のサンルーム、1901年頃撮影。左頁、下：メイン・ホール、1901年頃撮影。本頁、上：居間の暖炉を見る。本頁、下：主寝室。姿見は窓の間にあり、左右に対のブラケット照明が設けられる。後ろの壁面に大きな薔薇のステンシルが描かれ、横にミドルバックのラダーバック・チェアが置かれている。後のヒル・ハウスと居間や主寝室の構成は類似している。

House for an Art Lover
1901

芸術愛好家の家
1901

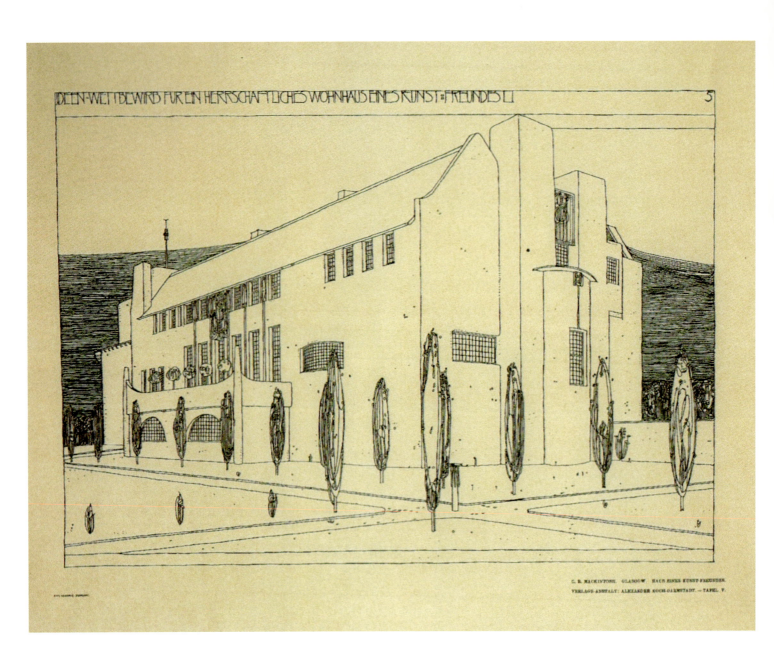

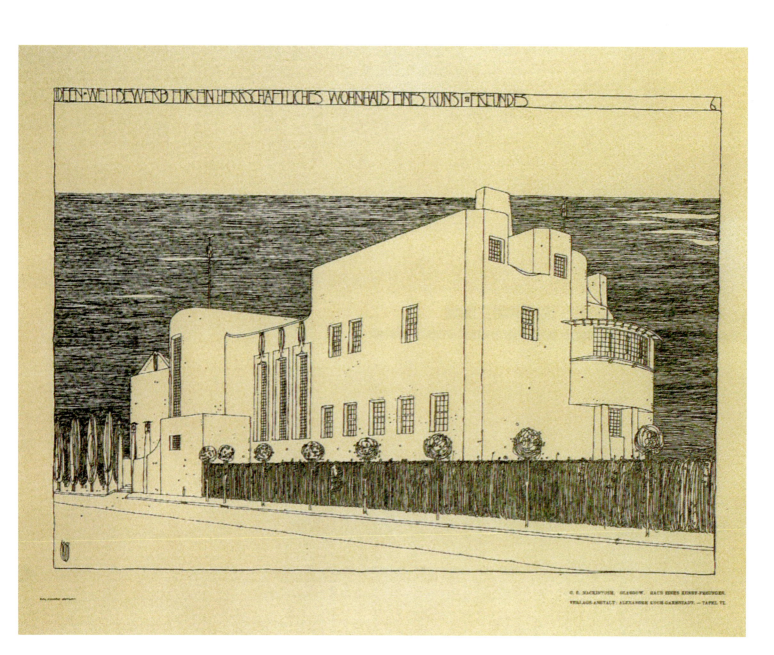

Opposite: Perspective view toward northwest, Meister Der Innenkunst *(1901), p. 6. Drawings on pp. 66–69 courtesy of The Hunterian, University of Glasgow. This page: Perspective view toward southwest,* Meister Der Innenkunst *(1901), p. 5.*

左頁：北西向パースペクティヴ図、『Meister Der Innenkunst』(1901) 6頁より。本頁：南東向パースペクティヴ、『Meister Der Innenkunst』(1901) 5頁より。

This page: Dining room perspective, Meister Der Innenkunst *(1901), p. 14.*
Opposite: Drawing and music room perspective, Meister Der Innenkunst *(1901), p. 7.*

本頁：ダイニング・ルームのパースペクティヴ、『Meister Der Innenkunst』(1901) 14頁より。右頁：居間とミュージック・ルームのパースペクティヴ、『Meister Der Innenkunst』(1901) 7頁より。

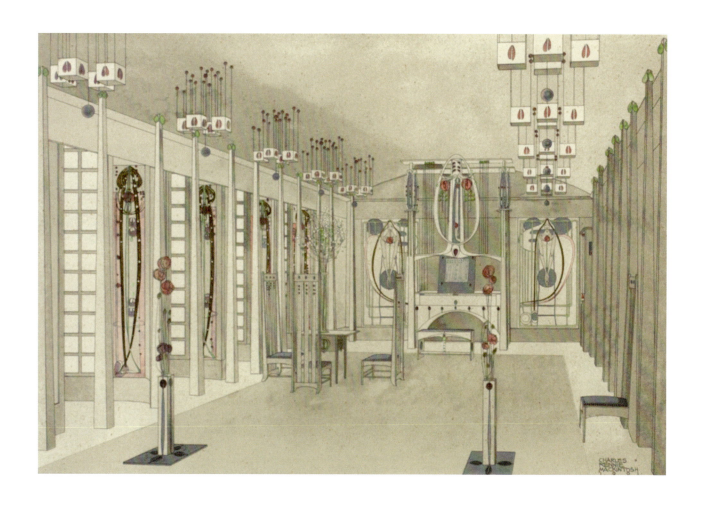

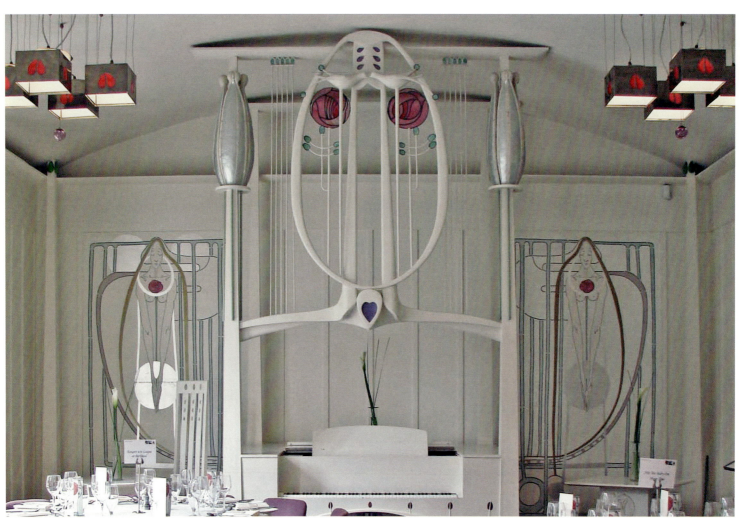

The Dawn of Modern Residential Architecture

In 1902, Charles Rennie Mackintosh's project House for an Art Lover was published as a 14-page color lithograph edition portfolio, along with works by Mackay Hugh Baillie-Scott of England, Leopold Bauer of Germany, Eero Saarinen of Finland, and others, by Alexander Koch, a publisher from Darmstadt, Germany.

The competition for the proposed house was originally solicited in the December 1900 issue of *Innendekoration*, a monthly interior design magazine, which asked the public to submit proposals for ideas for the new century.

While Mackintosh's proposal was not selected – it lacked the required number of perspective drawings – his modern design was highly acclaimed and won both a special award and the second-highest cash prize. The missing drawings were later added and published as a portfolio.

This proposed residence was conceived as an ideal house that would realize the principles of Mackintosh's architecture. In the drawing room, located in the center of the house, a built-in organ was designed to integrate a form of invisible music, through the amplifying its ornamental quality in a way that visually harmonizes with the rhythm of its living space. It was a bold proposal for a lifestyle that expresses its aesthetic quality through a stately dining room of furniture, lighting, and tableware, and a double-height hall with a gallery.

At the same time, Mackintosh's residence at Windy Hill (pp. 58–65) was completed, and The Hill House (pp. 12–49), a modern 20th-century residence that Mackintosh considered ideal, was planned and built in the Glasgow suburb of Helensburgh.

The idea of having a music room in the competition proposal was directly applied to the alcove of the drawing room of The Hill House, where a piano incorporated music into the daily life of the house.

Translated by Darryl Jingwen Wee

Opposite, top: Drawing and music room. The artistic space is created through the ornamental rhythm of the built-in organ, the wall painted motifs, and furnishings that mimick roses in vases. Photo by Jean-Pierre Dalbéra / flickr. Opposite, bottom: Dining room. The built-in furniture and furnishings of the interior use dark tones to create a modern and calm space. Photo courtesy of Getty Images. This page: This competition proposal was realized in 1990 in Bellahouston Park on the outskirts of Glasgow, by architect and Mackintosh researcher Andy McMillan. It currently functions as a café and event space. Photos courtesy of Hiroaki Kimura.

モダン住宅の始まり

1902年、ドイツ、ダルムシュタットの出版者であるアレクサンドル・コッホにより、イングランドのマッケイ・ヒュー・ベイリー・スコット、ドイツのレオポルド・バウアー、フィンランドのエーロ・サーリネン等と共に、シリーズ版の一つとして、マッキントッシュのプロジェクト、芸術愛好家の家は14枚綴りのカラー・リトグラフ版ポートフォリオとして出版された。

元々はインテリア月刊誌『Innendekoration』の1900年12月号で公募された、新世紀におけるアイディア提言を求めたコンペの住宅案であった。

マッキントッシュのコンペ案は、要求図面の透視図が不足していた為、当初選外となったが、そのモダンなデザインは高い評価を受け、特別賞を受賞、2番目に高い賞金を得る。その後不足していた透視図が追加され、ポートフォリオとして出版された。

この住宅案は、マッキントッシュの建築理念が追及された、理想的住宅であったはずである。住宅の中心となる居間には、造付けのオルガンがデザインされ、目に見えない音楽までもを生活空間にとり込み、リズムと協奏するように装飾性を増幅させ、そして、家具類照明から食器までを含めた重厚なダイニング、ギャラリーのある2層に吹き抜けたホール等、最大限に美意識を高めた住まい方を提案した大胆な案である。

丁度その頃に、ウィンディー・ヒル（58～65頁）が完成し、マッキントッシュが理想とした住宅としては、実際にグラスゴー郊外、ヘレンズバラに20世紀のモダン住宅となるヒル・ハウス（12～49頁）が計画・建設されることとなる。

コンペ案のミュージック・ルームのアイディアは、ヒル・ハウス居間のアルコーヴにピアノが置かれ、生活に音楽をとり込む空間として生かされた。

左頁、上：居間、ミュージック・ルーム。造付けのオルガンの奏でるリズムと壁面にくまなく描かれた装飾、そして家具のような花瓶に生けられた薔薇などが芸術的空間を演出する。左頁、下：ダイニング・ルーム。室内装飾・造付け家具、家具など全体を暗い色調に統一し、シックな落ち着きのある空間に仕上げている。本頁：このコンペ案は、1990年グラスゴー市内外れベラヒューストン公園内に、建築家およびマッキントッシュ研究者のアンディ・マクミランによって実現された。現在は芸術イヴェントの会場やカフェなどとして使用される。

Artist's Town House
1899–1900

芸術家の都市住宅
1899〜1900

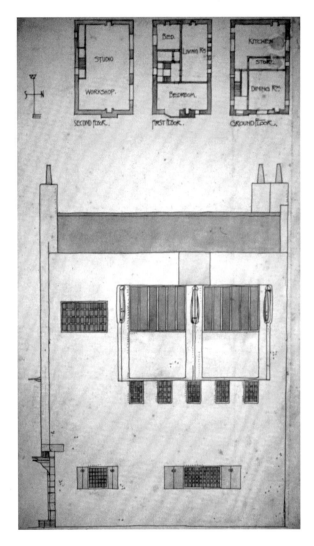
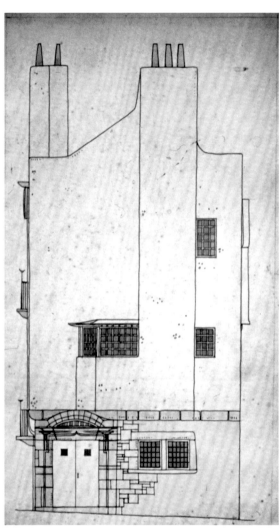

Charles Rennie Mackintosh planned several small houses that he had a particular liking for, leaving behind the proposals for 2 small artist's houses with a studio, around 1900. Both are designed as compact 3-storey urban houses for a small urban family. Each house features a dining room and kitchen on the ground floor, a bedroom and living room on the second floor, and a single-room studio on the third floor. On top of that, Artist's House and Studio in the Country, has a courtyard and backyard connected to the living room on the ground floor, and a studio on the second floor. It is also possible that these homes were proposed for Mackintosh and his wife, Margaret, as they married around this time.

Mackintosh also proposed 4 gate lodges, small houses for guards, for his client Hugh Brown Collins's Auchinbothie estate near Windy Hill (pp. 58–65). Here, as in The Hill House (pp. 12–49) and the small guard houses for Scotland Street School (pp. 162–167), Mackintosh proposed the exterior walls and gate lodges as a single unit. However, the built structure was a square lodge in the shape of a rice paddy.

Mackintosh also designed Ploughman's Cottage, a small, 2-storey square house that was built on the edge of a pond for H. B. Collins in 1906. The cottage was subsequently enlarged in 1908, and the L-shaped structure was renamed The Clock. After a second addition, the now T-shaped building was renamed Mossyde (1913). This was Mackintosh's last residential work before he left Glasgow.

Translated by Darryl Jingwen Wee

Artist's House and Studio in the Country
1899–1900

芸術家の田園住宅兼スタジオ
1899〜1900

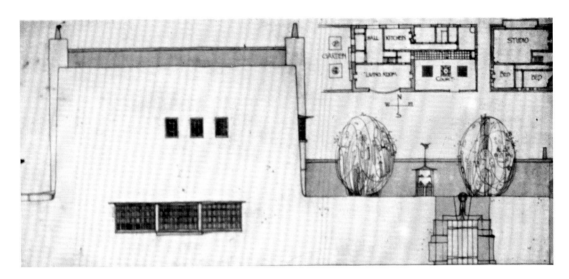

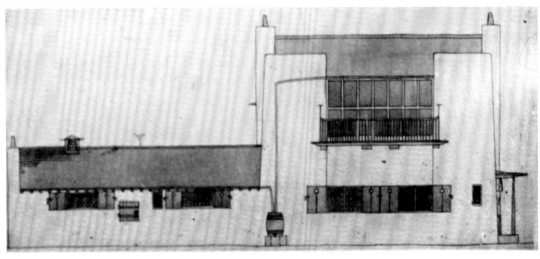

マッキントッシュは、いくつかの小さな住宅案を好んで計画している。1900年頃に、スタジオのある小さなアーティスト住宅案を残している。この2つの住宅は、一方は地上階にダイニングとキッチン、2階に寝室と居間、3階にワンルームのスタジオを配した、3層の狭小地の都市住宅案と、他方はコートヤードのある住宅案であり、ここには地上階に居間と繋がるコートヤードとバックヤード、2階に寝室とスタジオを設けている。どちらも小さな都市型の夫婦家族の小住宅であろう。丁度この頃、マッキントッシュとマーガレットが結婚していたため、その新居案とも考えられる。

またウィンディ・ヒル（58〜65頁）の近郊に、ヒュー・ブラウン・コリンズのオーチェンボシー邸に守衛の為の小さな住宅ゲート・ロッジを4提案行っている。ここでもマッキントッシュは、ヒル・ハウス（12〜49頁）やスコットランド・ストリート・スークル（162〜167頁）の守衛の為の小さな住宅同様に、外壁塀とゲート・ロッジを一体に繋ぐデザインを提案していた。しかし、最終的に建設されたのは、田の字型の正方形ロッジであった。

また1906年にはH・B・コリンズのために池のほとりに建つ農夫のコテージ、正方形2層の小さな住宅のデザインを行っている。その後このコテージは、1908年に増築されL型平面のクロックと称され、そして2度目の増築ではT型平面のモッサイド（1913）と称された。マッキントッシュがグラスゴーを離れる前、最後の住宅作品である。

Opposite: Artist's Town House. Entrance is located east to the townhouse, with the hall, dining room, and kitchen on the ground floor, the living room and bedroom on the second floor, and the studio with a high ceiling on the third floor. North elevation and floor plans (left). East elevation (right). Drawings on p. 72 courtesy of Glasgow School of Art. This page: Artist's House and Studio in the Country. Entrance is located west to the house, with the hall, living room, and dining room arranged in an L-shape around the courtyard on the ground floor, and the bedroom and large studio on the second floor. The courtyard is designed around 2 trees and a birdhouse. South elevation and floor plans (top). North elevation (bottom). Drawings on pp. 73–75 courtesy of The Hunterian, University of Glasgow.

左頁：芸術家の都市住宅。東立面に玄関口があり、地上階にはホール・ダイニング・キッチン、2階には居間・寝室、3階にはワンルームの天井の高いスタジオが配される。北立面図、各階平面図（左）。東立面図（右）。本頁：芸術家の田園住宅兼スタジオ。西に玄関口があり、地上階にはホール・居間・ダイニングが中庭を中心にL型に配され、2階には寝室と広いスタジオが配される。中庭には2本の樹木と鳥の巣箱がデザインされている。南立面図、各階平面図（上）。北立面図（下）。

Auchenbothie Gate Lodge
Kilmacolm, United Kingdom 1901–1902

オーチェンボシーのゲート・ロッジ
英国、キルマコーム　1901〜1902

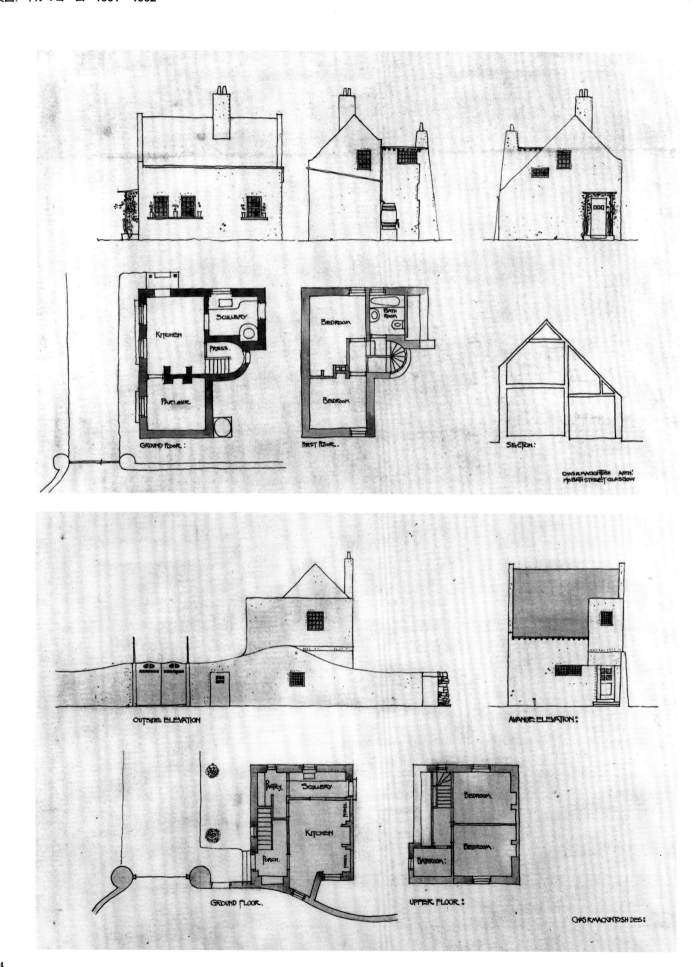

Opposite, top: Plan, elevation and section of the proposed stand-alone gate lodge. Opposite, bottom: Plan, elevation and section of the proposed gate lodge with integrated boundary wall. This page, top: Plan, elevation and section of the final design implementation for stand-alone gate lodge. This page, bottom: Plan, elevation and section of the proposed gate lodge with integrated gate.

左頁、上：独立住宅案。平立断面図。左頁、下：外壁一体案。平立断面図。本頁、上：独立住宅型、実施案。平立断面図。本頁、下：門一体案。平立断面図。

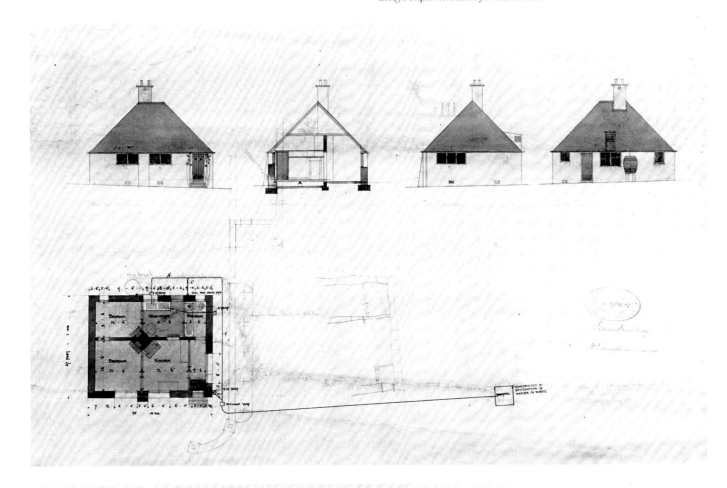

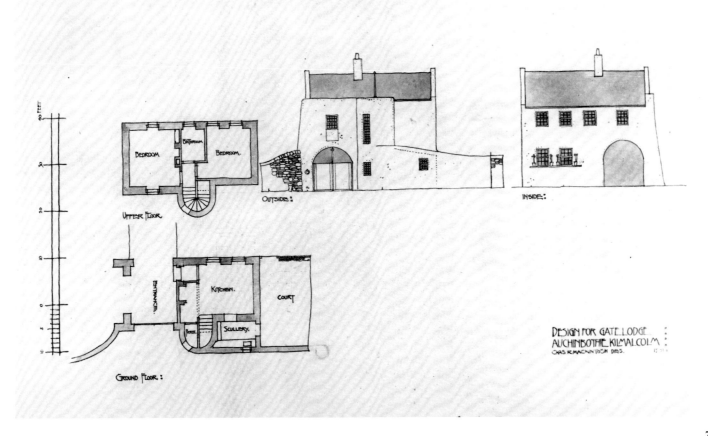

インテリア

Mackintosh House
Glasgow, United Kingdom 1900, 1906, 1981

マッキントッシュ自邸
英国、グラスゴー　1900、1906、1981

A Japanese flair

The flat at 120 Mains Street was Charles Rennie Mackintosh's personal residence, his new home following his marriage in 1900 to Margaret MacDonald, one of his greatest influences, an artist, and a member of The Glasgow Four. A Victorian-style interior remodel, the project marked Mackintosh's departure from the Arts and Crafts and art nouveau styles, as well as the peak of the avant-garde's prominence in Europe. In 1990 he was invited to the Vienna Secession, and the interior of his own residence was published in *The Studio*. A careful look at the photographs featured in this magazine reveals an interior with a Japanese flair. Above the fireplace in the center of the drawing room, which seems to have been the most elaborate design element of the new house, small Japanese prints in square white frames are matched with a piece of pottery that resembles a tea bowl, while a ukiyo-e woodblock print is hung on the wall across the room. Flowers arranged in vases recall Japanese ikebana, a way of enjoying plants and trees that differs from the propriety dictated by Western conventions. The interior of the room features Japanese-style wooden walls with exposed timber pillars, deftly adorned with attached columns and horizontal beams. Painted white, these columns and beams imbue the surface of the wall with an ornamental sensibility, creating a unique worldview. Unlike the somewhat ponderous, heavy-boned, cat-foot, front-legged furniture of the period – a trademark of Mackintosh's own furniture and chairs – this combination of slender, delicate boards and bars, pierced open carvings and horizontal footrest bars, and decorative features that resemble family crests evoke traditional Japanese furniture and techniques.

When the couple moved from this flat on Mains Street to a terrace house on Southpark Avenue in 1906, they brought this interior, with its white fireplace and built-in furniture, with them. An opening between the 2 spaces of the drawing room recall the continuity of Japanese-style rooms, while the bay window resembles a Japanese *engawa*. While this terrace house has been demolished, the original Japanese-style interior, with its fireplace and furnishings, has been reproduced and preserved in the Hunterian Art Gallery at the University of Glasgow, along with other furniture that Mackintosh designed and used.

Charles and Margaret's taste for Japan was evident even before they settled into their new home. Hanging on the wall of Charles's bedroom was an ukiyo-e woodblock print, as well as a stencil of a woman in a kimono, while fans adorned the fireplace in the drawing room of Margaret's Dumbarton Castle home.

Mackintosh often depicted women in kimonos in his paintings, and the cabinet furniture he designed for the children at Windy Hill (pp. 58–65) took the form of kimonos with the sleeves stretched out. The symbolic disk at the front of the Glasgow School of Art (pp. 116–151), which resembles a steel fence ornament, calls to mind the cross guard of a sword, or a crest. Like the Japanese *kamon* (crest), the disk is a symbol that renders geometric and natural forms such as flowers, leaves, butterflies, and birds in an abstract way and becomes ornamentation on buildings, tools, and clothing.

Ukiyo-e woodblock prints are a well-known Japanese influence on Impressionist painters, but Japanese art might be said to have similarly affected Western architecture. At first, Japanese art and design were incorporated into the aestheticism movement that began in the 1860s and 1870s, and were gradually taken up and absorbed by the new generation, including Mackintosh, in the 1900s. Mackintosh understood the use of the Japanese style by Edward William Godwin and James MacNeill Whistler, and appears to have been influenced both directly and indirectly by the architects and painters he admired.

Although this Japanese influence would gradually fade during Macintosh's later years, it generated his design ideas and served as the catalyst for his sensibilities around 1900 when he was most in the limelight. It also seems likely that Japanese art played an important role in his spatial designs.

The white, abstracted interior space of Mackintosh's own residence, 120 Mains Street Flat, may have triggered his breakthrough into modern architecture.

Translated by Darryl Jingwen Wee

Phase 1: 120 Mains Street, 1900
Phase 2: Terrace House on 78 Southpark Avenue (originally 6 Florentine Terrace), 1906
Phase 3: Preserved as Mackintosh House in The Hunterian Gallery, University of Glasgow, 1981

フェーズ 1：120メインズ通りのフラット 1900
フェーズ 2：サウスパーク・アヴェニュー（元はフロレンティン・テラス6番）のテラスハウス 1906
フェーズ 3：現在グラスゴー大学付ハンタリアン・ギャラリー内にマッキントシュ・ハウスとして再現保存 1981

pp. 77: Reassembled drawing room at The Hunterian, University of Glasgow. Mackintosh House is a representative work of the joint design by Mackintosh and Macdonald. Photos on pp. 77–84 courtesy of Hiroaki Kimura. pp. 78–79: Drawing room. The high-backed white chairs are stenciled with floral motifs, while small Japanese prints in square white frames sit on the mantelpiece. Silver-plated brass light fixtures are used throughout the house. Opposite, top: Drawing of the entrance door of 78 Southpark Avenue (1906). Drawings on p. 81 courtesy of The Hunterian, University of Glasgow. Opposite, bottom: Ground-floor and second-floor plan of 78 Southpark Avenue (1906, original scale: 1/96). The entrance hall, cloakroom, dining room, and kitchen are located on the ground floor, the study and drawing room on the second floor, and the master bedroom on the third floor.

77頁：グラスゴー大学のハンタリアン・ギャラリーにて再現された居間。マッキントッシュ邸は、マッキントッシュとマクドナルドの共同設計の代表作品である。78～79頁：居間。背もたれの高い白い椅子にはステンシルの花のモチーフが施され、マントルピースには額縁に入った日本人形が置かれている。真鍮製の銀メッキの照明器具は、家中至るところで使われている。右頁、上：サウスパーク・アヴェニューの玄関ドアの図面（1906）。右頁、下：サウスパーク・アヴェニューの地上階・2階平面図（1906年4月、原図縮尺：1/96）。地上階には玄関ホール、クローク、ダイニング、キッチンが、2階には二間続きの書斎と居間が、3階には主寝室が配される。

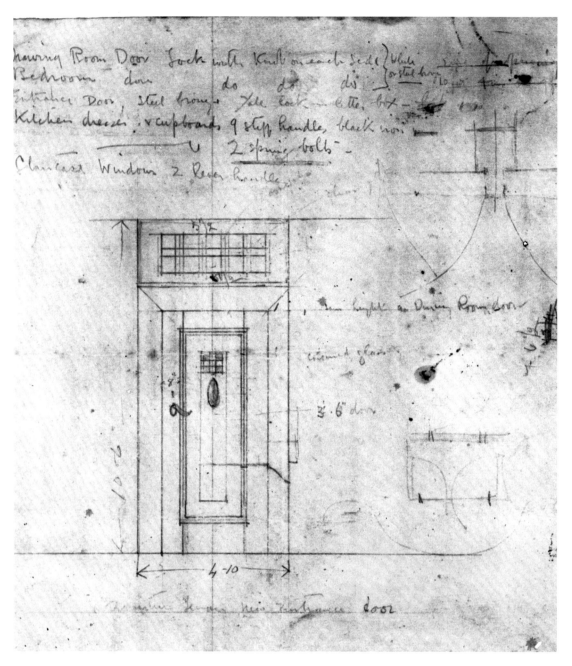
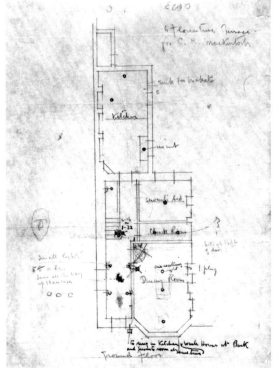
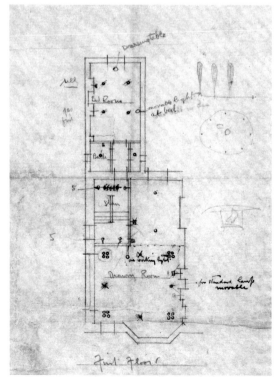

日本趣味

120メインズ通りのフラットは、マッキントッシュの自邸である。彼が最も影響を受けたアーティストおよびザ・フォーのメンバーであったマーガレット・マクドナルドとマッキントッシュが結婚し、それにともう新居であった。この建物は、ヴィクトリア様式のものでその室内を改装している。アーツ・アンド・クラフツとアール・ヌーヴォー様式からの、マッキントッシュの離別と転換を示す作品でもある。アバンギャルドとして、最もヨーロッパで注目をあびていた時期であり、1900年にはウィーンの分離派展に招待されていた。同年、自邸のインテリアを『スタジオ』誌に発表している。掲載写真を注意深く見ると、日本的趣味の伺えるインテリアで、この新居の最もデザインに神経を注いだと思える居間のその中心にある暖炉の上には、白い正方形の額に入った小さな日本の版画と茶碗のような陶器が対に飾られ、壁には浮世絵が掛けられている。花瓶に生けられた花を見ると、西欧従来の作法と異なり草木を楽しむ日本の生け花のようである。室内のインテリアは、壁面を日本風の真壁構造の木造建築のように付け柱と付け長押を巧妙にあしらい、それを白く塗り、壁面を装飾的に表現し、独自の世界観を創造している。

そして、マッキントッシュ家具や椅子の特色である、当時の重量感のある骨太で猫足の掘りのがっちりとした家具とは異なり、細身で華奢な板材と棒材を組み合わせ、透かしや貫き施し、家紋を遇うような装飾は、日本の伝統的な家具・道具類に通じるように思える。

1906年に彼らは、メインズ通りのフラットからサウスパーク・アヴェニューのテラスハウスに移り住むのだが、白い暖炉や造付け家具など内装も共に移設している。そして、居間の長押を回しオープンに2室をつなぐ開口も、和室の続き間のようであり、縁側のようなベイウィンドウのとり方も日本的である。その後このテラスハウスもとり壊されるが、オリジナルの暖炉や家具の装飾は残され、現在グラスゴー大学付属ハンタリアン・ギャラリーに、彼がデザインし愛用した家具とともに再現保存され、その日本的趣のインテリアは残されている。

マッキントッシュとマーガレットの日本趣味は、新居をかまえる以前から伺えた。マッキントッシュの寝室には、暖炉上の壁に浮世絵が掛けられ、壁には着物を着た女性のステンシルが描かれていたし、マーガレットの住まいであったダンバートン・キャッスルの居間の暖炉にも扇が飾られていた。

そして、マッキントッシュの絵には、しばしばキモノを着た女性が描かれたし、また、ウィンディー・ヒル（58〜65頁）の子供の為にデザインされたキャビネット家具は、袖を拡げたキモノ型である。また、グラスゴー美術学校（116〜151頁）の正面に施された鋼製フェンスの装飾のようなシンボリックな円盤は、刀の鍔のようであり、紋のようにも見える。それは、日本の紋と同様に、幾何学形態や花・葉・蝶・鳥などの自然のかたちを抽象化したシンボルで、それを装飾的に建物や道具、衣類などに用いている。

浮世絵などの日本の影響は、印象派の画家たちについてよく知られているが、同様に日本美術が西欧の建築家たちにも影響を及ぼしたと言える。はじめ日本の影響は、1860〜70年代から始まる唯美主義運動の中にとり込まれ、1900年代のマッキントッシュを含む新しい世代に徐々に引き継がれ吸収されたと考えられる。マッキントッシュは、エドワード・ウィリアム・ゴードウィンやジェームズ・マクニール・ホイッスラーによる日本風の利用をよく理解し、直接・間接的にも、彼が賞賛した建築家や画家達を通し影響されたと考えられる。

晩年は、徐々にその影響は失われるが、日本美術は、彼が最も脚光をあびた1900年前後のデザイン発想源、そして感性の起爆材であり、恐らくその空間造形にも重要な役割を果たしていたと考えられる。

自邸であったメインズ・フラットの白く抽象化され具現化したインテリア空間は、モダン建築への突破口となるきっかけとなった作品であろう。

pp. 82–83: Bedroom. Both the bed and cheval mirror are made of oak painted in white with a floral motif. The silver-plated hammered brass panel hung above the fireplace was created by Macdonald. This page, top left: Dining room. This room contains the first high-backed chairs designed for Argyle Street Tea Rooms. The sideboard was the first piece of furniture Mackintosh designed for himself. This page, top right: Entrance hall. The transom window above the door filling the entrance with daylight is designed by Mackintosh, while a hammered lead frame mirror hanging on the wall in front is created by Macdonald. Mackintosh also designed another version of the coat stand used in Argyle Street Tea Rooms for their home. Opposite: Portrait of Margaret Macdonald. Photos on pp. 85–87 courtesy of T. & R. Annan and Sons. text

82〜83頁：寝室。ベッドも自立鏡もオーク材を白く塗ったもので、花のモチーフが組み込まれている。暖炉上の銀メッキ打ち出し真鍮パネルはマクドナルドによる。本頁、左上：ダイニング・ルーム。この部屋にはアーガイル・ストリート・ティールームのためにデザインされた初のハイバック・チェアが置かれている。サイドボードはマッキントッシュがはじめて自分のためにデザインした家具である。本頁、右上：玄関ホール。玄関を光で満たすためにマッキントッシュがデザインした長窓の前にはマクドナルドが製作した鉛製の打ち出し鏡が吊るされている。アーガイル・ストリート・ティールームで使われていたコートスタンドの別バージョンを自宅で制作している。右頁：マーガレット・マクドナルド。

Margaret Macdonald (1864-1933)

Margaret Macdonald was a great influence on Charles Rennie Mackintosh and the only one with whom he would collaborate. The embroideries and painted decorations in The Hill House (pp. 12–49) and Miss Cranston's Tea Rooms (pp. 92–109) were works created by Macdonald. Some years older than Mackintosh, she is considered to be his main source of inspiration. Her influence is apparent in the feminine elegance of Mackintosh's designs.
The pre-modern art nouveau featured feminine motifs of nature, women, and children. Jessie Morris, a muse of William Morris and Dante Gabriel Rossetti, was the inspiration behind their designs. Similarly, Macdonald is thought to have been Mackintosh's muse. One can imagine how the women of Glasgow School of Art were themselves inspired. The school symbolized a new era as it was an institution of higher education for women.
Mackintosh clearly admired Macdonald's artistic genius. In his excellent painting, *The Harvest Moon* (1892), an angelic muse appears silhouetted against the moon. Right around then, Mackintosh meets Macdonald and breaks his engagement to Jessie Keppie, John Keppie's sister. The white furniture of Glasgow School, a departure from the Arts and Crafts movement, is said to have been inspired by a plaster torso created by Macdonald.
Macdonald's family moved from Manchester to Glasgow in the 1880s. The family was not an artistic one and her father was an engineering consultant. Mackintosh remodeled the living room of Macdonalds' family home, Dunglass Castle (1899), and designed the white fireplace that preceded his and Margaret Macdonald's residence, 120 Mains Street Flat.

Hiraoki Kimura

マーガレット・マクドナルド（1864〜1933）

マーガレット・マクドナルドは、最もチャールズ・レニー・マッキントッシュに影響を与え、そして唯一、作品上でコラボレーションのできた人物である。ヒル・ハウス（12〜49頁）やティールーム（92〜109頁）に見られるエンブロイドや絵画装飾は、マクドナルドの作品である。年上であったマーガレットは、恐らくマッキントッシュの精神的支えとなったのだろう。またマッキントッシュによるフェミニンなエレガントなデザイン性の背後には、常にマクドナルドの存在が伺える。
プレモダンであったアール・ヌーヴォーのモチーフには、自然や女性と子供しか登場せず、フェミニンなデザインである。ジェシー・モリスは、ウィリアム・モリスとダンテ・ゲイブリエル・ロセッティのマドンナ的存在であり、デザイン創作の源泉であった。同様にマクドナルドは、マッキントッシュのミューズ的存在であったと考えられ、そしてグラスゴー美術学校の女性達の存在は、デザイン・インスピレーションであったと想像できる。また、当時の美術学校は、新時代を象徴する女性の高等教育機関でもあった。
マッキントッシュの秀作である、《The Harvest Moon》（1892）には、月明かりを背後に、天使のようなマドンナが現れる。丁度その頃にマクドナルドが現れ、マッキントッシュはジェシー・ケペ（ジョン・ケペの妹）との婚約を解消している。そして、アーツ・アンド・クラフツからの離別となったグラスゴー派の白い家具は、マクドナルドによる石膏トルソーからの着想とされる。マッキントッシュは、マクドナルドを天才と賞賛していた。
マクドナルドの家族は、1880年代にマンチェスターからグラスゴーに移り住んでいる。父親はエンジニア・コンサルタントであり、芸術一家ではなかった。マッキントッシュは、マクドナルドの実家ダングラス・キャッスル（1899）の居間を改装し、彼らの新居となった120メインズ・フラットに先駆けて白い暖炉のデザインを手掛けている。

木村博昭

This page: 120 Mains Street Flat interior.

本頁：120メインズ・ストリート・フラット内観。

Hous'hill
Glasgow, United Kingdom 1904–1910

ハウス・ヒル
英国、グラスゴー　1904〜1910

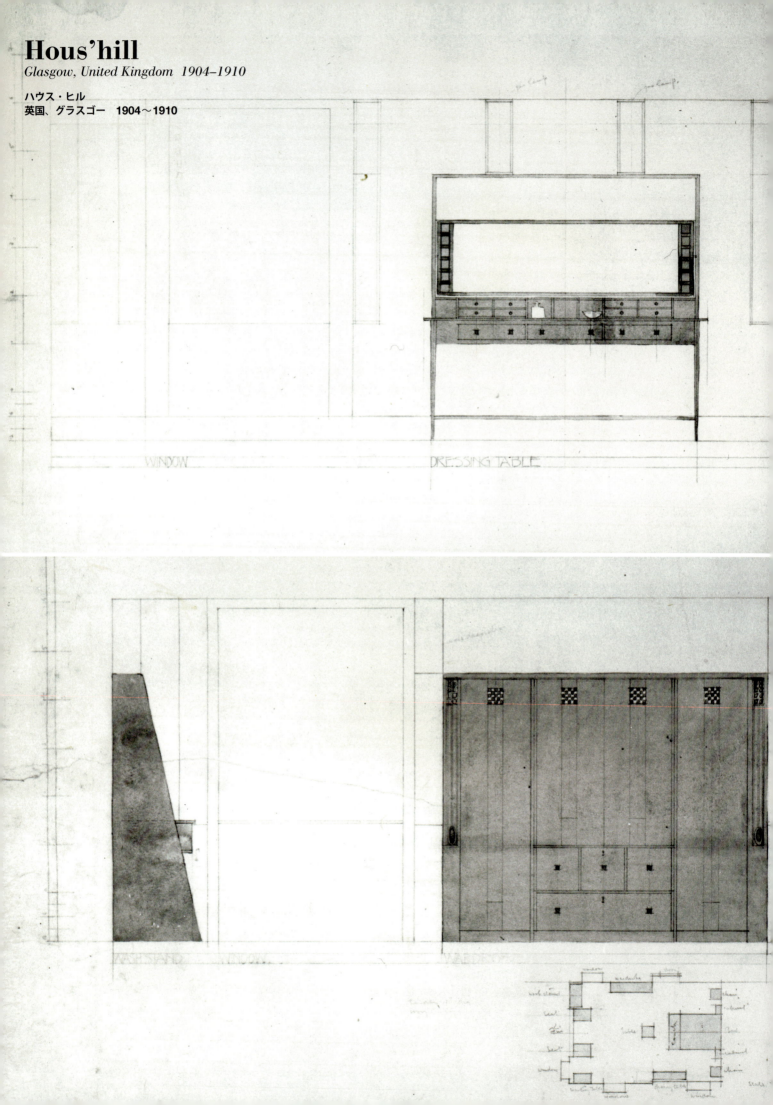

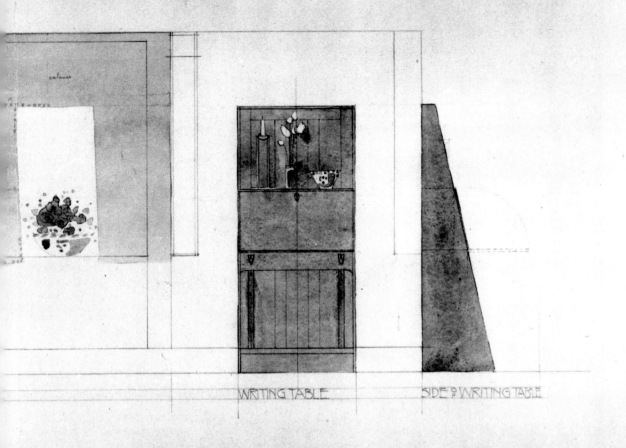

WRITING TABLE — SIDE OF WRITING TABLE

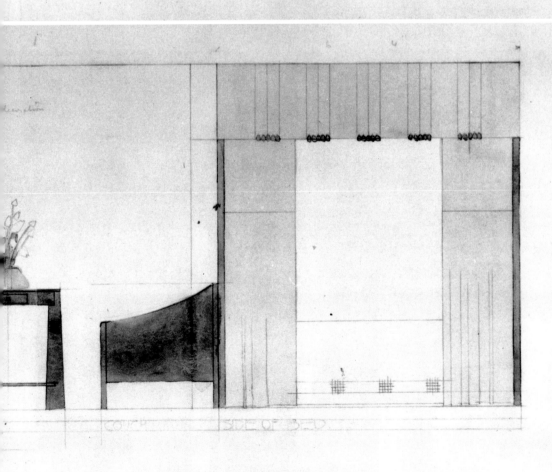

SIDE OF BED

Hous'hill was the residence of Catherine Cranston, a good friend and confidante of Charles Rennie Mackintosh. She lived in the house from 1905 until about 1920, when the interior was unfortunately demolished due to a resale and fire.
A well-known local entrepreneur with sharp business acumen and a taste for the modern, Cranston owned Miss Cranston's Tea Rooms, which Mackintosh also designed (pp. 92–109). Hous'hill, dated from the 17th century, was remodeled by Mackintosh, and enlarged with new interior decor for the hall, billiard room, and card room, as well as the living area with dining and music rooms, 2 blue bedrooms and a white bedroom, and many built-in furnishings.
Here, Mackintosh seems to have consciously attempted to divide the public space for entertaining guests from the private space for the family by manipulating the heights of the ceilings. In contrast to the hall, dining, and billiard rooms, which generally take on the volumes of Victorian architecture of the time, the ceiling height of the blue and white bedrooms, which are private spaces, has been kept abnormally low without compromising spaciousness. Judging from the photos that survive, the ceiling is almost within reach if a person of average stature extends their arms upward.
Meanwhile, the height of the living area with the music room where the family gathers is treated as an in-between zone. This living area where the family can spend time together has a piano, as does The Hill House. It consists of a single, continuous space, although it is separated by a white screen decorated with a brilliant semicircular arc that creates a rhythmic, musical space that might otherwise feel monotonous.
Today, only a few pieces of furniture remain, and the contrasting black and white furniture of the white bedroom is on permanent display at Musée d'Orsay in Paris.

Translated by Darryl Jingwen Wee

pp. 88–89: Blue Bedroom elevations. Drawings courtesy of The Hunterian, University of Glasgow. Opposite, top: Blue Bedroom. Photo courtesy of Year Book of Decorative Art MCMVII, The Studio, London Paris & New York, 1907. Opposite, bottom: Furniture exhibited at Central Gallery of Glasgow School of Art. From left to right: White Bedroom. Dressing table. Bed and low-backed chair. Photos on p. 90 bottom courtesy of Hiroaki Kimura. This page, bottom: Portrait of Catherine Cranston. Photo courtesy of T. & R. Annan and Sons.

Miss Cranston's Tea Rooms

クランストン夫人のティールーム

Urban Commons and the Dawn of Salons

It is no exaggeration to say that British tearoom culture began in Glasgow at the end of the 19th century when Miss Cranston's Tea Rooms were located on Argyle Street, Buchanan Street, Ingram Street, and Sauchiehall Street, all of them within the city center. These tearooms were places where local residents encountered sophisticated, modern interior design and experienced a kind of urban commons where everyone could freely enjoy conversation. While salon culture had been about social gathering places for men, tearooms were social spaces that catered to women.

Willow Tea Rooms, in particular, were establishments owned by Miss Cranston where Mackintosh's artistic design techniques were successfully applied to a commercial space.

Willow Tea Rooms (now Mackintosh at the Willow) face Sauchiehall Street. (Sauchiehall means "willow alley" in Scottish, and Mackintosh used a willow motif in the interior.) The front façade of the existing 4-storey building, which originally faced the street, was redesigned with bulging side windows and a white façade in a seeming allusion to the international style. A new tearoom naturally lit by a lattice-ceilinged gallery was also added to The Back Saloon.

Today, in the restored Willow Tea Rooms, guests can settle into a Mackintosh chair, sip tea, and relive the splendor of early 20th-century Glasgow. The interior space on the second floor, surrounded by the silver and purple high-backed chairs of The Salon de Luxe, features a sprinkling of glass beads and Margaret Macdonald Mackintosh's paintings. The tableware, other furnishings, and even the graphics on the menu boards have all been conceived in a truly magnificent design that befits a lady. One can well imagine that this was one of the most fashionable places in Europe in its heyday.

Later, in 1917, an art deco tearoom named The Dug-Out, a reference to the war years of World War I, was added to the basement.

Sites of experimentation for Charles Rennie Mackintosh, the interiors of Miss Cranston's Tea Rooms allowed the architect to work as a versatile designer, conceptualizing spaces for new lifestyles, from interiors, wall decorations, and interior furnishings to light fixtures, furniture, and tableware. This was arguably a place where he was able to expand the framework of the architect as a designer, exerting an influence on the interests of the modernist architects who came after him in the design of interior and furniture for all aspects of life, as well as specific design techniques for the human body.

Translated by Darryl Jingwen Wee

都市のコモン、サロンの始まり

英国に於けるティールーム文化は、19世紀末のグラスゴーから始まったと言っても過言でない。クランストン夫人のティールームは、グラスゴー中心街の骨格を成した、アーガイル通り、ブキャナン通り、イングラム通り、ソキホール通りにあった。ティールームは市民が身近にハイセンスなモダン・インテリアに触れ、空間体験をすることのできた場であり、そして誰しもが自由に会話を楽しめた都市のコモンであったと想像できる。サロン文化はこれまで男性社会の社交場であったが、ティールームは、特に女性の社交場であった。

特にウィロー・ティールームは、一連のティールームの中でも、マッキントッシュによる空間演出の芸術的デザイン手法が、商業スペースに応用され、成功した作品である。ウィロー・ティールーム（現マッキントッシュ・アット・ザ・ウィロー）は、ソキホール通りに面している。ソキホールとは、スコットランド語で柳の小径を意味し、それにちなんでウィローと名付けられ、インテリアも柳をモチーフにデザイン展開されていた。通りに面した4階建ての既存建築の正面ファサードを、インターナショナル・スタイルを暗示する膨らみのある横窓と白いファサードの建築に一新させている。バック・サルーンとして、自然光の射し込む格子天井のギャラリーのあるティールームが新たに増設された。

現在、ウィロー・ティールームは、修復され、ティールームとして市民に公開されている。ここでマッキントッシュの椅子に腰掛け、お茶を飲むと、時を超えて当時のグラスゴーの華麗な世界が実体験として蘇る。2階にあるサロン・デラックスでは、シルバーとパープルのハイバック・チェアに囲まれたインテリアが展開し、女性達が宝石で着飾るようにガラス玉の装飾が散りばめられ、マーガレットの絵画が描かれ、テーブルウェアなど調度品、そしてメニュー板のグラフィックに至るまでトータルなデザインで構想され、その輝きは、実に華麗であり貴婦人達に似合う空間である。ここは当時のヨーロッパでも最もファッショナブルな場所であったであろうと想像できる。

その後1917年に、第一次世界大戦下をもじりザ・ダグアウト（防空壕）と名付けられたアール・デコの秀作となるティールームが地下に増設された。

一連のティールームのインテリアは、建築家であったマッキントッシュが、多才なデザイナーとして活躍できた場であり、インテリア・壁面装飾・造付け家具・照明器具・家具・テーブルウェアに至る、新たな生活様式にかかわる空間演出の実験場であったと考えられる。それは、デザイナーとしての建築家の枠を広げ、その後のモダニズムの建築家達の生活全般にかかわるインテリアや家具デザイン等への興味や、身体にかかわる具体的なデザイン手法に影響を与えたであろうと思われる。

Willow Tea Rooms
Glasgow, United Kingdom 1902–1904

ウィロー・ティールーム
英国、グラスゴー　1902〜1904

p. 92: The Front Saloon. Photos on pp. 92–100 courtesy of Hiroaki Kimura unless otherwise specified. p. 93: Entrance on the north façade along Sauchiehall Street. This page, top: Queue is formed at the entrance. The teamrooms are as lively as it were since its opening in 1903. This page, bottom: Window seats facing Sauchiehall Street. Opposite: The Baldacchino, an ornament used for worship, is suspended from the ceiling. The Back Saloon is visible behind the lattice back cashier's chair. Photo from Dekorative Kunst no. 8, 1905, p. 260.

92頁：フロント・サルーン。93頁：メイン・エントランスのある北ファサード、ソキホール通りから見る。本頁、上：正面エントランスを見る。訪れた人々で賑わう建設当時の様子。本頁、下：ソキホール通りに面する窓側席。右頁：バルダッキーノという礼拝に使われる華飾りが空中に飾られている。奥にバック・サルーン、中央に格子背のキャッシャーズ・チェアを見る。

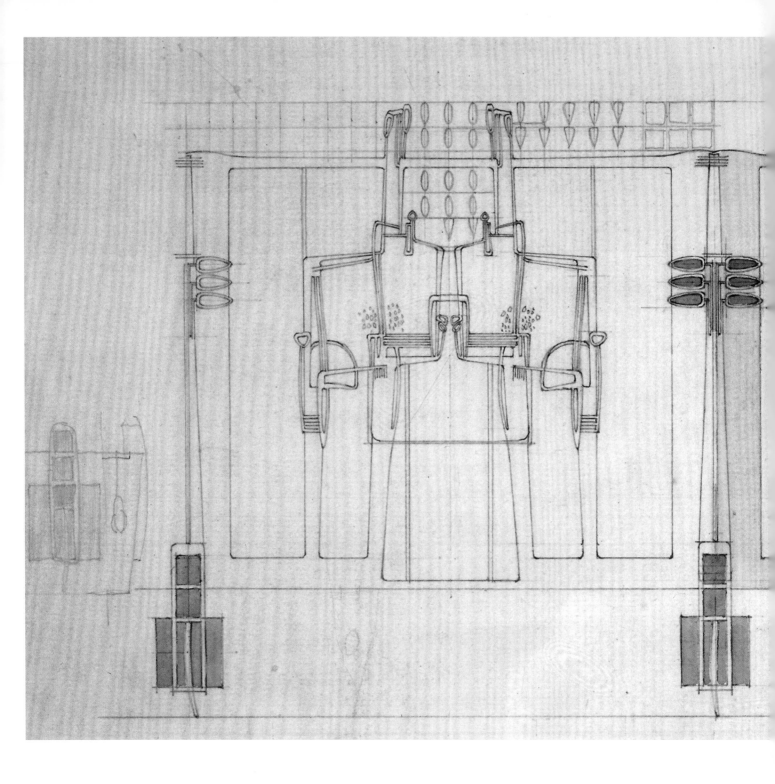

This page, top: Design for a decorative relief frieze. Drawing courtesy of The Hunterian, University of Glasgow. Opposite, bottom left: The Front Saloon on ground floor. Opposite, bottom right: Original plastered fireplace and wall decorations in The Front Saloon.

本頁、上：レリーフ装飾フリーズのデザイン。右頁、左下：地上階フロント・サルーン。右頁、右下：フロント・サルーンにある漆喰仕上げのオリジナル暖炉と壁面装飾。

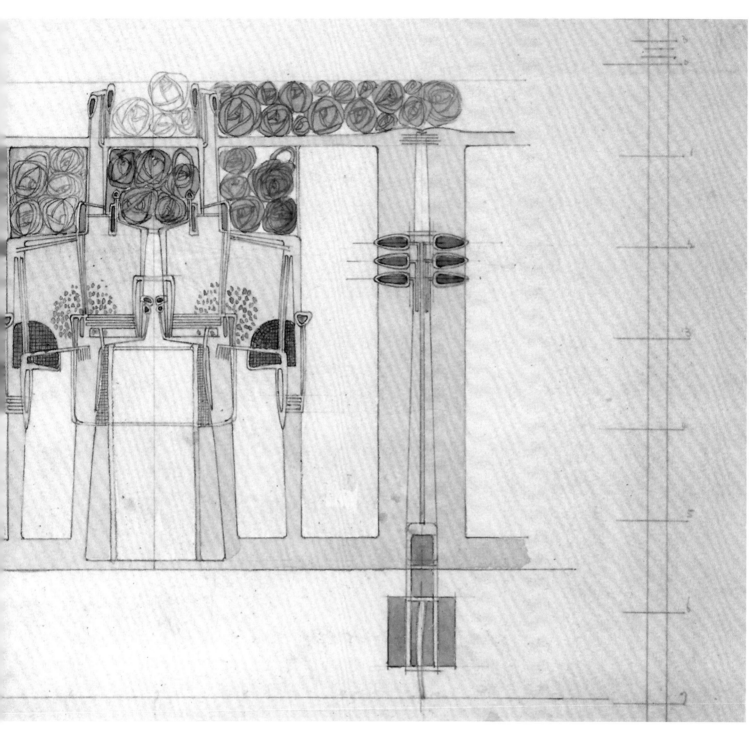

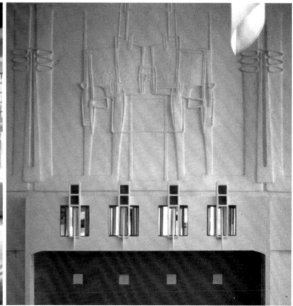

This page: The Salon de Luxe on the second floor overlooking Sauchiehall Street.

本頁：ソキホール通りを見渡せる2階のサロン・デラックス。

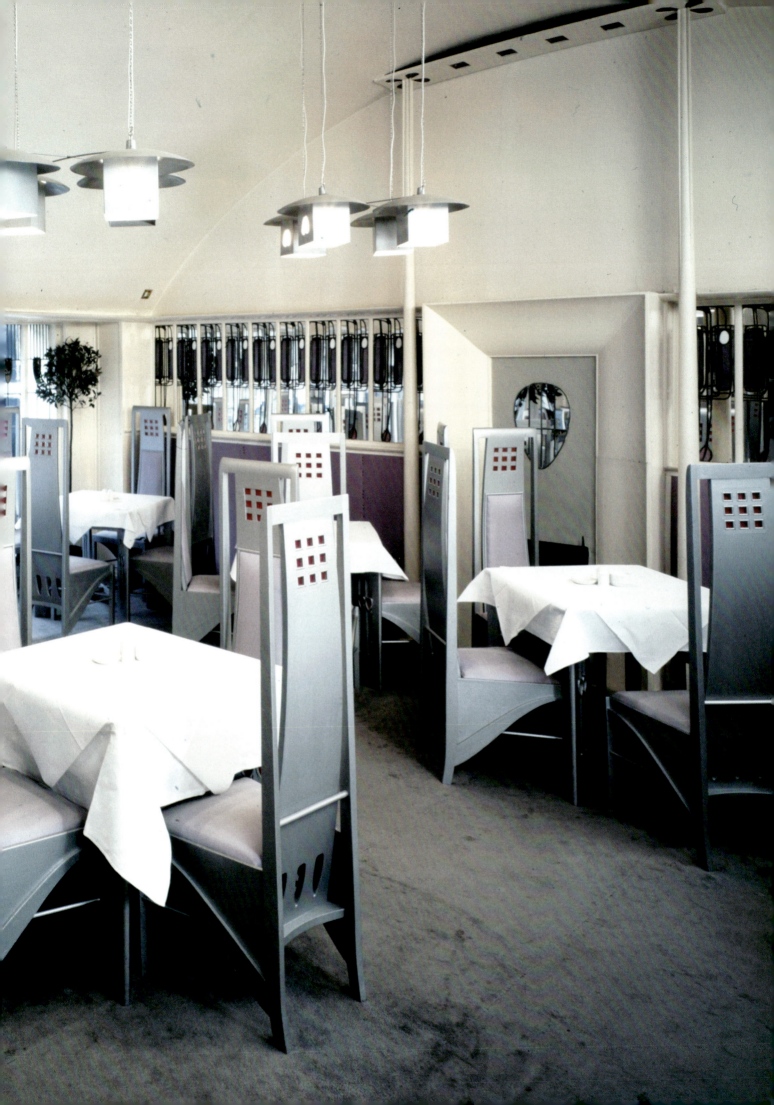

Opposite, top left: Cashier's chair with a curved lattice back (1904, oak, ebonized, horsehair upholstered seat, 118.9 × 94 × 41 cm). The chair, placed between The Front and Back Saloons, functions as a partition separating the 2 saloons. The lattice back incorporates a willow motif, and has a storage space for money and receipts beneath its seat. Opposite, top right: The Back Saloon armchair (1903, oak, ebonized, horsehair upholstered seat, 72.8 × 55.3 × 45.4 cm). Also used in the smoking room, the armchair has a simple structure constructed out of solid wood with punctuated holes. Opposite, right, middle: Ladder back chair (1903, oak, ebonized, woven rush seat, 104.8 × 45.5 × 41.2 cm). The chair, along with a box armchair, is used in The Front Saloon and The Gallery on the ground floor. The ladder back was later reinforced by a bar along the rear side of the top slat. Opposite, bottom: Reproduction of the yellow settee from Mackintosh's drawing. This page: Elevation of Cashier's chair. Drawing courtesy of Hida Takayama Museum of Art.

左頁、左上：キャッシャーズ・チェア（1904、オーク材エボニッシュ仕上げ、馬毛張りの座面、18.9×94×41cm）。カーヴした格子背の椅子。地上階フロント・サルーンとバック・サルーンの間に置かれ、2つのサロンを隔てるパーテーションとして機能した。格子は柳をモチーフにデザイン。シートをもち上げるとお金や領収書を入れる収納スペースがある。左頁、右上：バック・サルーンの肘掛椅子（1903、オーク材エボニッシュ仕上げ、馬毛張りの座面、72.8×55.3×45.4cm）。スモーキング・ルームでも使用。穴の抜かれた板材を組み合わせたような単純な構造の椅子。左頁、右中：ラダーバック・チェア（1903、オーク材、エボニッシュ仕上げ、い草編みの座面、104.8×45.5×41.2cm）。地上階フロント・サルーンとギャラリーで箱型の肘掛け椅子と並べ用いられた。ラダーバックの最上部は後に補強のため横材が付加されている。左頁、下：ドローイングに描かれたイエロー・セトの再現品。本頁：キャッシャーズ・チェア立面図。

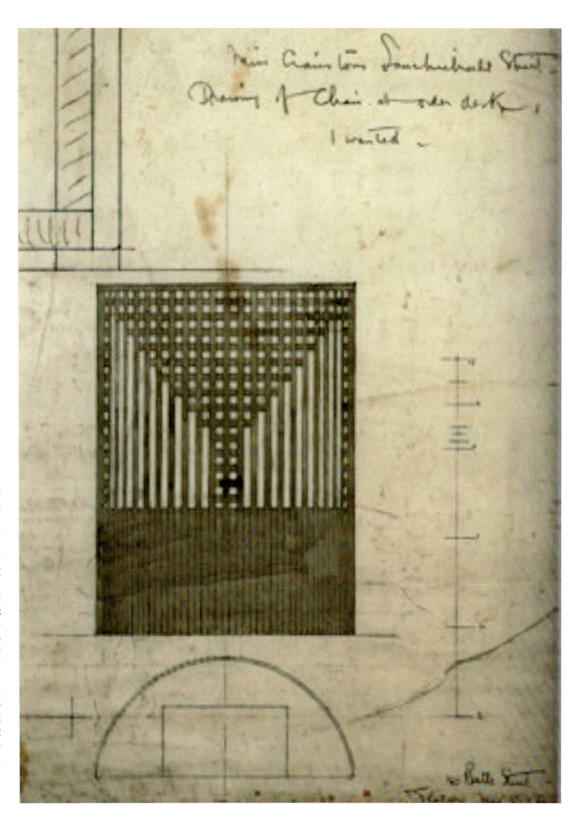

The Dug-out
1916–1917

ダグアウト
1916〜1917

This page, bottom left: Design drawing of the Victory Monument above The Dug-Out fireplace. This monument commemorates the Allied victory in World War I. The Japanese ensign is depicted next to the American flag. Drawings on pp. 102–103 courtesy of Glasgow School of Art. pp. 102–103, top: North interior elevation. pp. 102–103, bottom: West interior elevation.

本頁、左下：ダグアウト暖炉上部の戦勝記念碑のデザイン画。第一次世界大戦の連合国の戦勝を記念して設けられた。日本の軍艦旗がアメリカ国旗の横に描かれている。102〜103頁、上：北壁面展開立面図。102〜103頁、下：西壁面展開立面図。

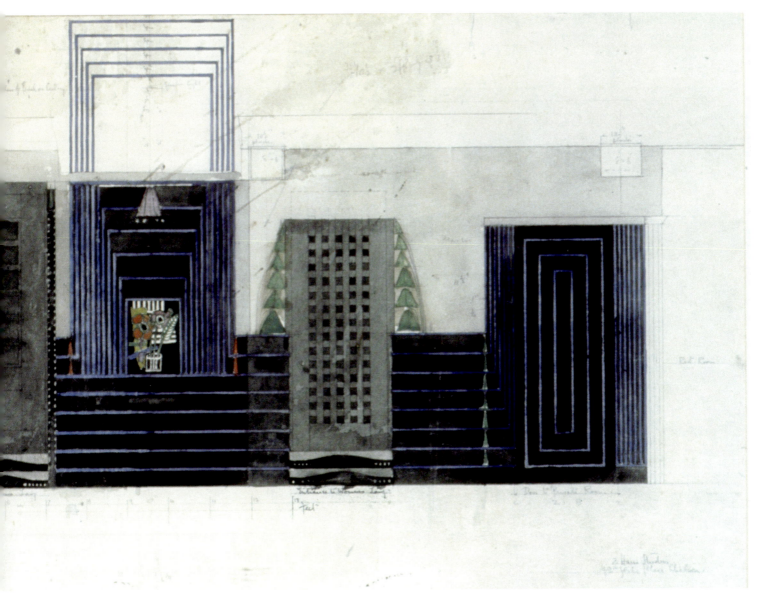

Buchanan Street Tea Rooms
Glasgow, United Kingdom 1895–1896

ブキャナン・ストリート・ティールーム
英国、グラスゴー　1895〜1896

This page, bottom left: Buchanan Street Tea Room was the first Cranston Tea Room Mackintosh was involved with. He would go on to work on a series of other projects throughout his life. The building was designed by Edinburgh architect George Washington Browne, with its interiors by George Walton. Mackintosh created wall stencils for the Ladies' Tea Room, Lunch Room, and Smoking Room, and designed part of its light fixtures. Photos on pp. 104–107 courtesy of T. & R. Annan and Sons. pp. 104–105: Stenciled wall painting of female figures in the Ladies' Tea Room on the second floor. Drawing courtesy of The Hunterian, University of Glasgow.

本頁、左下：ブキャナン・ストリート・ティールームは、マッキントッシュが最初にかかわったクランストン・ティールーム。その後生涯にわたって一連の仕事を手掛けることになる。建物はエジンバラの建築家ジョージ・ワシントン・ブラウン、内装はジョージ・ウォルトンが手掛けた。マッキントッシュは、レディース・ティールーム、ランチ・ルーム、スモーキング・ルームの壁面ステンシル・デザインと、いくつかの照明デザインを行なった。104〜105頁：2階レディース・ティールーム、女性像の壁面ステンシル画。

Argyle Street Tea Rooms
Glasgow, United Kingdom 1897–1898

アーガイル・ストリート・ティールーム
英国、グラスゴー　1897〜1898

This page: West part of the ground-floor Lunch Room in Argyle Street Tea Room. George Walton designed the interior, while Mackintosh did its furniture and light fixtures. Mackintosh also designed the Dutch Kitchen extension in 1905-1906.

本頁：アーガイル・ストリート・ティールーム地上階ランチ・ルームの西側。内装をジョージ・ウォルトンが行い、マッキントッシュは家具類と照明デザインを担う。1905〜1906年にはダッチ・キッチンの増築デザインを行う。

Ingram Street Tea Rooms
Glasgow, United Kingdom 1900–1901

イングラム・ストリート・ティールーム
英国、グラスゴー　1900〜1901

This page: Ingram Street Tea Rooms. Mackintosh started with the interior design of White Dining, Billiard, and Cloister Rooms in 1900, followed by Oak Room in 1907, Oval Room in 1909, and lastly Chinese and Cloister Rooms in 1911. Photo courtesy of The Hunterian, University of Glasgow.

本頁：イングラム・ストリート・ティールーム。 内装デザインは1900年のホワイト・ダイニング、ビリヤード、クロイスター・ルームに始まり、1907年のオーク・ルーム、1909年のオーヴァル・ルーム、1911年のチャイニーズ、クロイスター・ルームと続く。

Argyle Street Tea Rooms, Furniture

アーガイル・ストリート・ティールーム、家具

This page, left: High-backed chair with an oval headrest used in Dining Room (1897, dark stained oak, horsehair upholstered seat, 136 × 50.5 × 45.8 cm). It is the first high-backed chair designed by Mackintosh. Photos on pp. 108–109 courtesy of Hiroaki Kimura. This page, top right: Low-backed armchair used in Billiard and Smoking Room (1897, dark stained oak, 84 × 63 × 46 cm). This page, bottom right: Armchair (1897, dark stained oak, horsehair upholstered seat, 96.4 × 57.2 × 45.8 cm).

本頁、左：オーバル・バックレイルのあるハイバック・チェア（1897、オーク材ダークステイン仕上げ、馬毛張りの座面、136×50.5×45.8cm）。ダイニング・ルームで使われた。マッキントシュによる最初のハイバック・チェア。本頁、右上：肘掛のあるローバック・チェア（1897、オーク材ダークステイン仕上げ、84×63×46cm）。ビリヤード・ルーム、スモーキング・ルームで使われた。本頁、右下：肘掛け椅子（1897、オーク材ダークステイン仕上げ、馬毛張りの座面、96.4×57.2×45.8cm）。

Ingram Street Tea Rooms, Furniture

イングラム・ストリート・ティールーム、家具

This page, top left: High-backed dining chair used in White Dining Room (1900, dark stained oak, horsehair upholstered seat, 151 × 47.3 × 43.3 cm). This page, top right: Middle-backed dining chair (1900, dark stained oak, horsehair upholstered seat, 106.4 × 47.7 × 43.8 cm). This page, bottom left: Chinese Room chair (1911, ebony stained pine, horsehair upholstered seat, 82.4 × 43.8 × 40.7 cm). The back and apron of the chair are designed with a meander (thunder) pattern which recalls Chinese influence. This page, bottom middle: Low-backed chair used in Oak Room (1906, dark stained oak, woven rush seat, 70 × 40.6 × 35 cm). This page, bottom right: Low-backed chair used in Oval Room and the ladies restroom (1909, dark stained oak, woven rush seat, 72 × 40.6 × 34.5 cm).

本頁、左上：ハイバック・ダイニング・チェア（1900、オーク材ダークステイン仕上げ、馬毛張りの座面、151×47.3×43.3cm）。ホワイト・ダイニングで使われた。本頁、右上：ミドルバック・ダイニング・チェア（1900、オーク材ダークステイン仕上げ、馬毛張りの座面、106.4×47.7×43.8cm）。本頁、左下：チャイニーズ・ルーム・チェア（1911、松材エボニー仕上げ、馬毛張りの座面、82.4×43.8×40.7cm）。中国風のデザインに合わせ背と横木が雷文にデザインされた。本頁、中下：ロウバック・チェア（1906、オーク材ダークステイン仕上げ、草編みの座面、70×40.6×35cm）。オーク・ルームで使われた。本頁、右下：ロウバック・チェア（1909、オーク材ダークステイン仕上げ、草編みの座面、72×40.6×34.5cm）。オーヴァル・ルームと女性化粧室で使われた。

78 Derngate
Northampton, United Kingdom 1917–1920

78 ダンゲート
英国、ノーサンプトン 1917〜1920

After leaving Glasgow in 1914, Charles Rennie Mackintosh and his wife, the artist Margaret Macdonald Mackintosh, set up a studio in Chelsea, London. Although they were commissioned to build an apartment complex and a theater, neither of these projects advanced beyond a draft proposal.

Wenman Joseph Bassett-Lowke, the proprietor of a model maker, commissioned Mackintosh to renovate 78 Derngate as his new home following his marriage.

Compared to Mackintosh's previous works, this was an interior design project for a very small terrace house. Mackintosh worked on it with great energy and enthusiasm, however, treating it as a bona fide challenge, and once again he broke new ground with an avant-garde design. The strong primary colors and weighty feel of the house, representing a complete departure from the white, pale, and elegant Glasgow style of the past, create a highly polished interior and furnishings that showcase the abilities of a more mature and competent architect. The use of yellow plastic, a material that was still new at the time, as an inlay for the smoking cabinet also demonstrates a novel and innovative aspect of Macintosh's style.

78 Derngate is perhaps the only masterpiece of art deco residential architecture, which is exceedingly unique in England, a country that still favors more conservative, traditional styles. Today, the 78 Derngate interior has been restored to its original appearance and offers an experience of the art deco space of Mackintosh's later years in England.

Translated by Darryl Jingwen Wee

グラスゴーを去り、マッキントッシュとマーガレットは、1914年以降ロンドン、チェルシーにアトリエを構える。集合住宅や劇場の依頼を受けるがどれも計画案に終わり、実現には至らなかった。

78ダンゲートは、モデル・メーカーの経営者のウェンマン・ジョセフ・バセット＝ロークが、結婚後の新居として改装をマッキントッシュに依頼する。

これまでの作品と比べると極めて小さなテラスハウスのインテリア・プロジェクトであるが、マッキントッシュは、精力的かつ挑戦的にとり組み、再びアバンギャルドとしてデザインの新境地を開いた作品である。これまでの白く淡いエレガントなグラスゴー・スタイルとは離別した、強い原色と重厚感のある趣は、非常に完成度の高いインテリアと家具に仕上げられ、より成熟した力量の建築家像を示している。そして、当時まだ新素材であった黄色のプラスチック板を、象嵌のようにスモーキング・キャビネットに使用した、斬新な一面も示している。

恐らく78ダンゲートは、まだ保守的な伝統様式を好む英国内にあって、極めて特異であり、英国内では当時唯一のアール・デコの住宅の秀作だったであろう。

現在、この78ダンゲートのインテリアは当時のように再生保存され、イングランドでのマッキントッシュ空間の体験、また、英国内のマッキントッシュ晩年のアール・デコ空間が体験できる場所となっている。

pp. 110–111: Elevation of the staircase screen wall in the lounge hall. The screen features a wall stencil with the image of a late autumn forest in strong black and yellow colors. The stained glass, stand, and chairs are treated equally, each carefully designed. Drawing courtesy of The Hunterian, University of Glasgow. pp. 112–113: Compared to the feminine elegance in The Hill House, the guest bedroom in 78 Derngate projects a more masculine image. Photos on pp. 112–115 courtesy of The 78 Derngate Northampton Trust unless otherwise specified. Opposite: Lounge hall interior. This page, top: Art deco style lounge hall. This page, bottom: The bedroom furniture is now on display at The Hunterian, University of Glasgow. Photo courtesy of Hiroaki Kimura.

110〜111頁：ラウンジ・ホール、階段スクリーン・パネルの室内展開図。強い色彩の黒と黄色を基調に晩秋の森をイメージした壁面ステンシルが特徴的。ステンドガラス、スタンド、椅子を等価に扱いデザインを行なっている。112〜113頁：客用寝室、ヒルハウスのフェミニンな空間イメージと比べ、78ダンゲートの寝室はより男性的である。左頁：ラウンジ・ホール内観。本頁、上：アール・デコのラウンジ・ホール。本頁、下：現在寝室家具のセットはグラスゴー大学のハンタリアン・ギャラリーに再現展示されている。

115

Public Buildings

公共建築

Glasgow School of Art
Glasgow, United Kingdom 1896–1899, 1907–1909

グラスゴー美術学校
英国、グラスゴー　1896〜1899、1907〜1909

Charles Rennie Mackintosh emerged professionally at the young age of 27 when he won a competition to design a new building for Glasgow School of Art – the most important work of his life. Mackintosh studied there from the age of 16, designed its new building, and taught there until 1913, when he left Glasgow to spend his final years in southern France. It was here that he had important encounters with the school director Francis Henry Newbery, along with schoolmates James Herbert MacNair and sisters Margaret and Frances MacDonald, with whom he later formed a group of designers called The Glasgow Four and worked on the continent.

With this building Mackintosh forged a new style of architecture that broke away from traditional classical styles, focusing instead on functionality, the position and size of openings, and a rationality that determined the design features of buildings based on their necessity. It was a concrete example of an architecture that would become the forerunner of modernism that sought a new direction for the discipline.

Glasgow School of Art is also a powerful work that represents the most honest expression of the style and philosophy that underlie Mackintosh's architecture. After winning the design competition in 1896, the construction of the building was divided into 2 phases. The first phase (1897–1899) involved the construction of only the left half of the front of the building, and the new school building opened in late December 1899. The second phase (1907–1909) of construction for the right half began 10 years later. The entire building thus took 15 years to complete. The first phase consisted of curves and botanical elements in the art nouveau style. Mackintosh was at first sensitive to the influence of Charles Francis Annesley Voysey, William Burges, and Edwin Lutyens, and was quick to incorporate the design trends of the time into his architecture. During the second phase, Mackintosh's design ability increased with age, leading him to establish a design technique based on binary opposites, using negative and positive space to invert convex and concave forms, light and dark, and black and white, which demonstrated a great sense of originality inspired by contemporary architecture from the same period. In his late period, Mackintosh abandoned curvilinear design entirely, in favor of an art deco style that emphasized more mechanical and heavy geometric motifs.

A building connecting the eras that engendered 2 styles, Glasgow School of Art is a valuable specimen that preserves traces of the historical flow and design transition process during the 15 years that modernism developed out of the Victorian style.

pp. 120,140 translated by Darryl Jingwen Wee

p. 117: Front entrance. Photo by Shinkenchiku-sha. pp. 118–119: Northwest view. Photos on pp. 118–150 courtesy of Hiroaki Kimura unless otherwise specified. This page, top: East façade after the first phase of construction. The octagonal tower element is similar to that in Queen's Cross Church. This page, bottom: Sketch of the first phase that was published in the newspaper. Opposite: West extension completed in the second phase.

117頁：正面入口。118〜119頁：北西から見る。本頁、上：第一工期にできた東立面。八角形の塔状エレメントは、クイーンズ・クロス教会にも見受けられる。本頁、下：新聞で発表された第一工期スケッチ。右頁：第二工期にできた西側増築。

Competition Entry 1897

コンペティション提案 1897

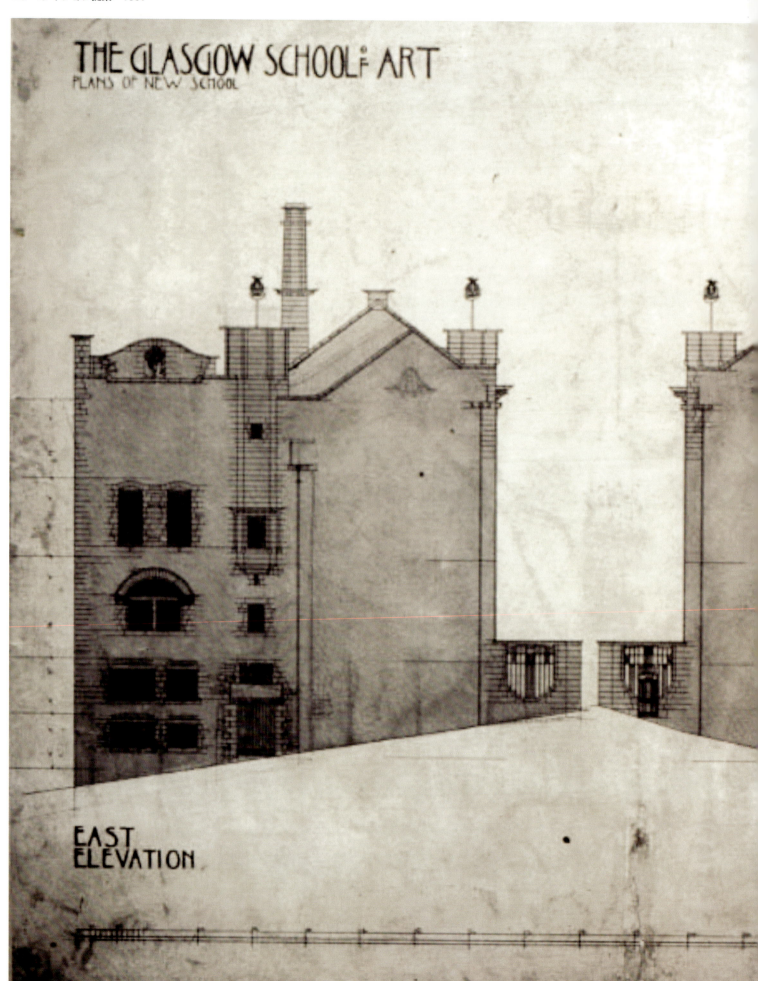

As-Built Drawings   1910

竣工図面　1910

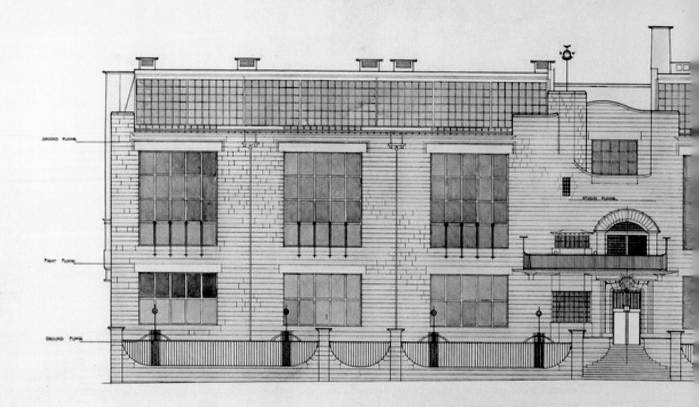

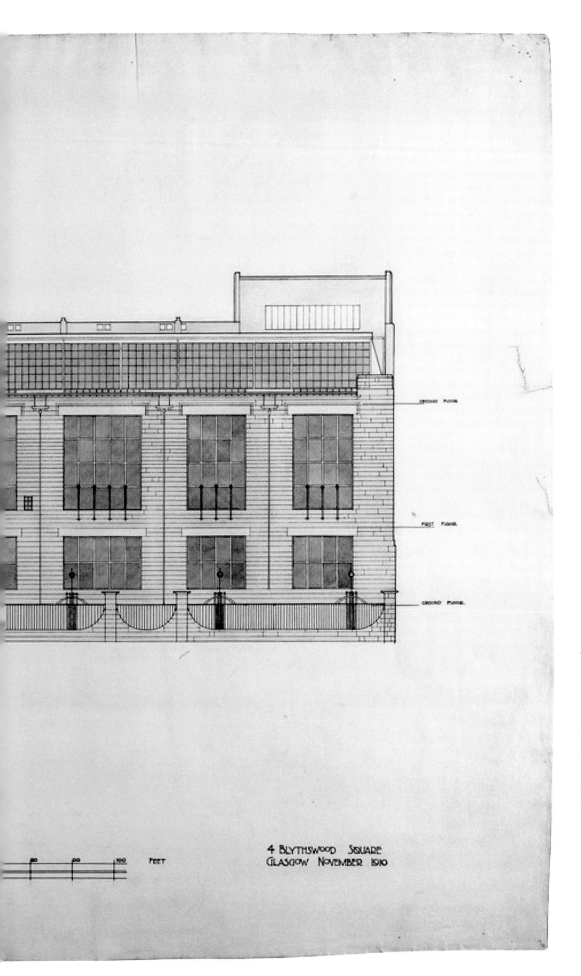

pp. 122–123: East (left) and west (right) elevations (March 1897, original scale: 1/96). With a 10-year gap between the competition and its realization, the constructed west façade is very different from its proposed design. Drawings on pp. 122–127 courtesy of Glasgow School of Art. This page: North elevation (November 1910, original scale: 1/96). In the second phase of construction, the art nouveau pitched roof built in the first phase was removed, and a flat-roofed attic studio was added to the top floor.

122〜123頁：東立面図（左）、西立面図（右）（1897年3月、原図縮尺：1/96）。10年の差があるコンペ提案と実現案で、西立面は大きく異なっている。本頁：北立面図（1910年11月、原図縮尺：1/96）。第二工期ではアール・ヌーヴォー期のデザインであった第一工期の勾配屋根をとり払い、平屋根のアティック・スタジオが最上階に増設された。

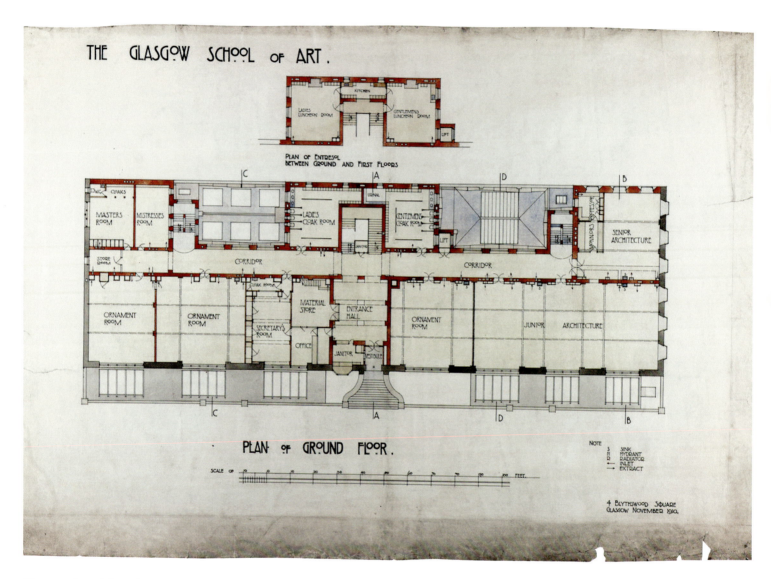

This page: Ground-floor plan (November 1910, original scale: 1/96). Opposite: Second-floor plan (November 1910, original scale: 1/96).

本頁：地上階平面図（1910年11月、原図縮尺：1/96）。右頁：2階平面図（1910年11月、原図縮尺：1/96）。

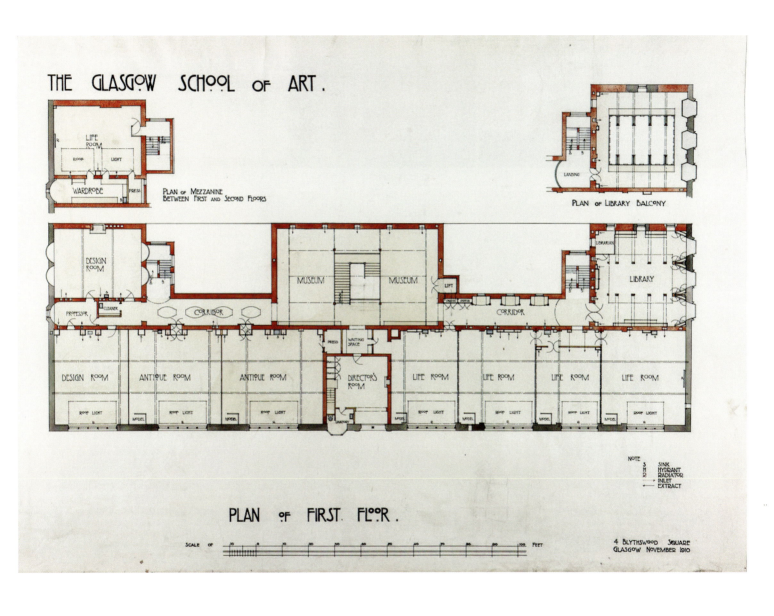

This page: East and west façades were designed 10 years apart. Opposite: Front entrance. The director's office is located on the mezzanine floor above the entrance, while the director's private studio is located on the upper floor. The entire front façade consists of elements such as balconies, bay windows, half-arched windows, and stair towers. Photo by Shinkenchiku-sha.

本頁：10年の間を空けてデザインされた東・西立面。右頁：正面入口。玄関上部中二階には学長室、その上階には学長の個人用アトリエが配されている。正面立面の全体はバルコニー・出窓・半円弧窓・階段塔など様々な要素で構成されている。

グラスゴー美術学校は、彼の生涯にかかわる最重要作品である。マッキントッシュは、16歳からここで学び、新校舎を創造し、そして、晩年グラスゴーを去る1913年まで、教鞭をとっていた。グラスゴー美術学校の学長、フランシス・ヘンリー・ニューベリーや、美術大学の仲間であった、ジェームズ・ハーバート・マクネイアー、マーガレットとフランシスのマクドナルド姉妹たちとの出会いは重要である。その後、彼ら4人はザ・フォーと呼ばれるデザイナー・グループを組織し、大陸で活動する。

マッキントッシュがその頭角を現すのは、27歳の若さでグラスゴー美術学校の新校舎の設計コンペに勝利し、従来の古典様式から抜けだし、開口部の位置や大きさなど、機能性や必要性にもとづく合理性によって建築デザインが決定される、新たな建築の在り方めざしたモダニズムの先駆けとなる建築を具現的に示した事にある。

この作品はマッキントッシュ建築の作風・理念が最も素直に表現された力作である。それは、コンペ設計（1896）に始まり、二期に工期を分け建設され、第一期（1897〜1899）は、正面の左側半分だけが建設され、1899年12月下旬に新校舎は開校した。その10年後に第二期工期（1907〜1909）が始まり、続いて右側半分が建設、15年間をかけて全体が完成する。第一期では、アール・ヌーヴォー様式にもとづく曲線や植物モチーフのエレメントが構成され、敏感にチャールズ・フランシス・アネスリー・ヴォイジーやウィリアム・バージェス、エドウィン・ラッチェンス等の影響を受けながら、逸早く時代のデザイン潮流を自分の建築にとり入れていた。第二期では年齢と共にデザイン力が増し、同時代の建築の影響から、よりオリジナリティを発揮した凸凹のように反転させたネガポジデザインや、光の明暗、黒白といった二元対比のデザイン手法を確立し、後期になると曲線的デザインは一掃され、機械的なモチーフや重厚な幾何学的モチーフのエレメントにより重点を置くアール・デコに至る。

グラスゴー美術学校は、2つの様式の時代を繋ぐ建物であり、ヴィクトリア様式から始まるモダニズムへと展開した15年間の歴史上の流れとそのデザイン変遷過程の痕跡をそのままに残した貴重な建築とも言える。

First Phase
1897–1899

第一期
1897〜1899

Opposite: The 2 small entrance doors opens up to a multi-layered interior space consisting of a semi-basement studio, 2 high-ceilinged studios, and an attic studio. This page, top: The front entrance lintel is ornamented with art nouveau style female figures and botanical abstractions. This page, bottom: Flight of stairs leading to the front entrance.

左頁：正面入口。小さな2枚の片開きの扉から入ると、内部には半地下スタジオ、天高の高いスタジオ2層分、そして最上階のアティック・スタジオが重層する空間が広がる。本頁、上：正面入口上部ディテール、アール・ヌーヴォー様式の植物と女性の石彫装飾。本頁、下：階段ブリッジを渡り建築に入る。

This page: Gallery hall in the center of the building. According to the records, the wood paneling of the hall was painted in green at the time of the school's opening. After, it was repainted dark brown. The hall is naturally well-lit by an extensve skylight. Opposite: Director's office, nearing completion circa 1900 without furniture or light fixtures. Photo courtesy of Glasgow School of Art.

本頁：建物中央のギャラリー・ホール。内装は木板を多用し、開校当時の記録によると緑に着色されていたが、のちに濃い焦茶に塗り直された。全面トップライトにより採光が確保される。右頁：学長室、1900頃の完成間近の様子。まだ家具や照明が整っていない。

This page: Director's office, photo taken in the 1980s.

本頁：学長室、1980年代撮影。

Second Phase, Working Drawings   1907

第二期、検討図面　1907

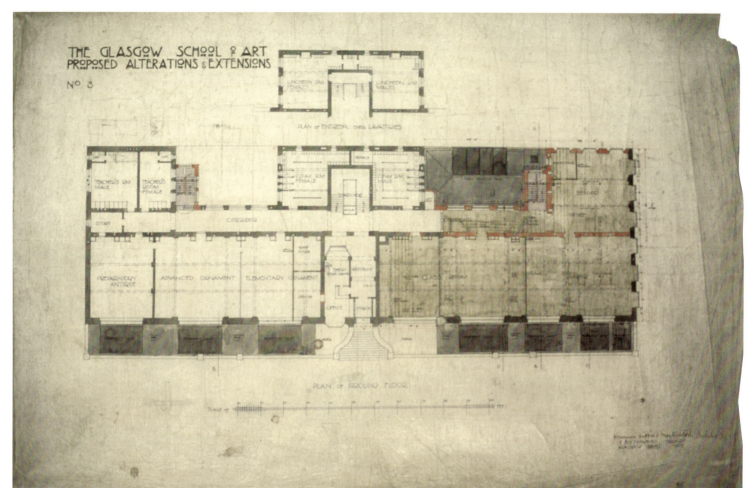

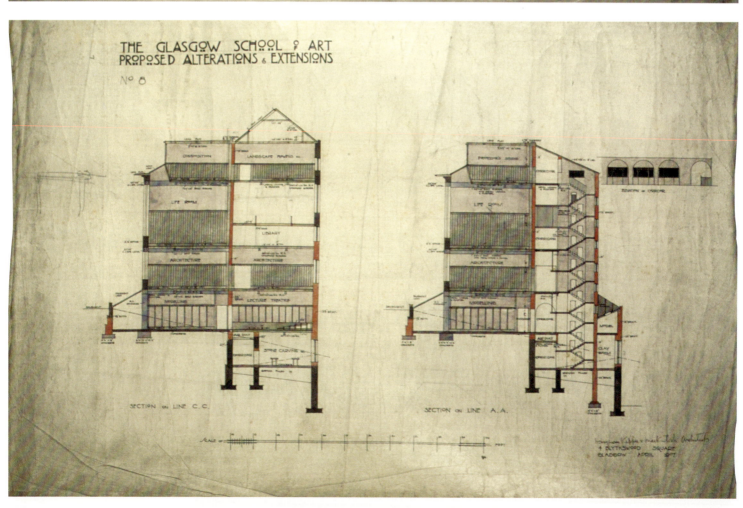

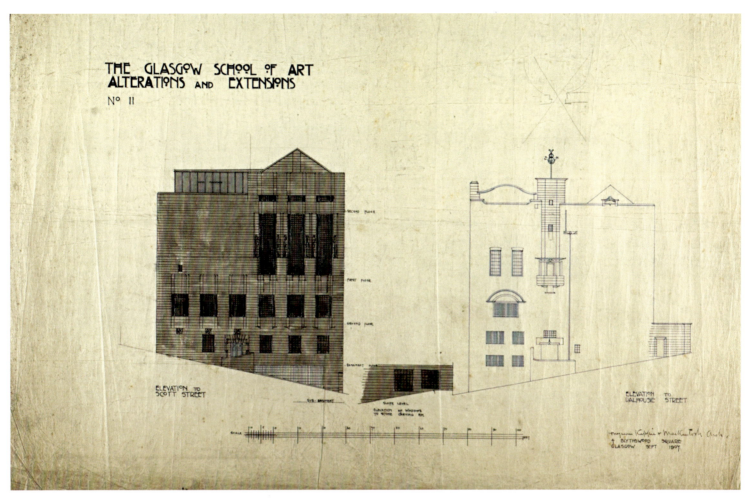
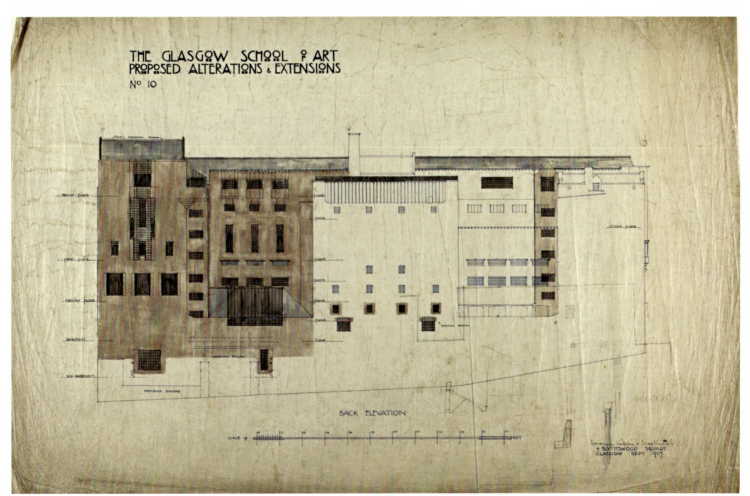

Second Phase, Construction Drawings for the Dean of Guild 1907

第二期、ディーン・オブ・ギルド用実施図面　1907

pp. 122-127, 136-139: At least 6 sets of drawings have been produced for Glasgow School of Art. Competition drawings (1896), first phase construction drawings for the Dean of Guild (1897), second phase design revision drawings for the university (1907), construction drawings for the Dean of Guild (1907), working drawings (1907), as-built drawings (1910).

122〜127、136〜139頁：グラスゴー美術学校のために少なくとも6セットの図面が製作された。コンペ図面（1896）、第一工期ディーン・オブ・ギルド用実施図面（1897）、第二工期大学用図面（1907）、ディーン・オブ・ギルド用実施図面（1907）、検討図面（1907）、竣工図面（1910）。

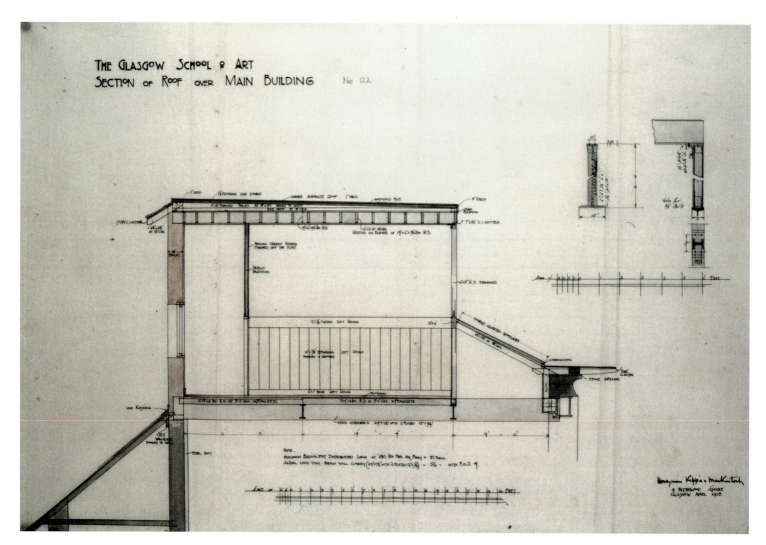

p. 136, top: Ground-floor plan (September 1907, original scale: 1/96). Drawings on p. 136 courtesy of Keppie Henderson Partners Architects. p. 136, bottom: Transverse section (September 1907, original scale: 1/96). p. 137, top: West (left) and east (right) elevations (September 1907, original scale: 1/96). Drawings on p. 137 courtesy of The Hunterian, University of Glasgow. p. 137, bottom: South elevation (September 1907, original scale: 1/96). This page: Detailed section of the attic studio's extension and renovation (April 1908, original scale: 1/12, 1/24). The pitched roof built in the first phase was replaced with a flat-roofed attic studio and skylight. In order to reduce the dead load added to the building, the extension was constructed using steel and timber frameworks. Drawings on pp. 138-139 courtesy of Glasgow City Archives. Opposite: Detailed section (June 1907, original scale: 1/24). The building comprises of different materials, stone on its façade, steel for the trusses, and concrete and wood for the floor.

136頁、上：地上階平面図（1907年9月、原図縮尺：1/96）。136頁、下：断面図（1907年9月、原図縮尺：1/96）。137頁、上：西立面図（左）、東立面図（右）（1907年9月、原図縮尺：1/96）。137頁、下：南立面図（1907年9月、原図縮尺：1/96）。本頁：最上階スタジオ、増築改修断面詳細図（1908年4月、原図縮尺：1/12、1/24）。第一工期の勾配屋根をとり払い、平屋根のアティック・スタジオの増築改修とトップライトの増設を行った。建築荷重の軽減のため、新たな鉄骨柱梁、木組みによる増築とされた。右頁：断面詳細図（1907年6月、原図縮尺：1/24）。ファサードは石造、トラス梁は鉄骨造、床はコンクリート・木造と、混構造でつくられた。

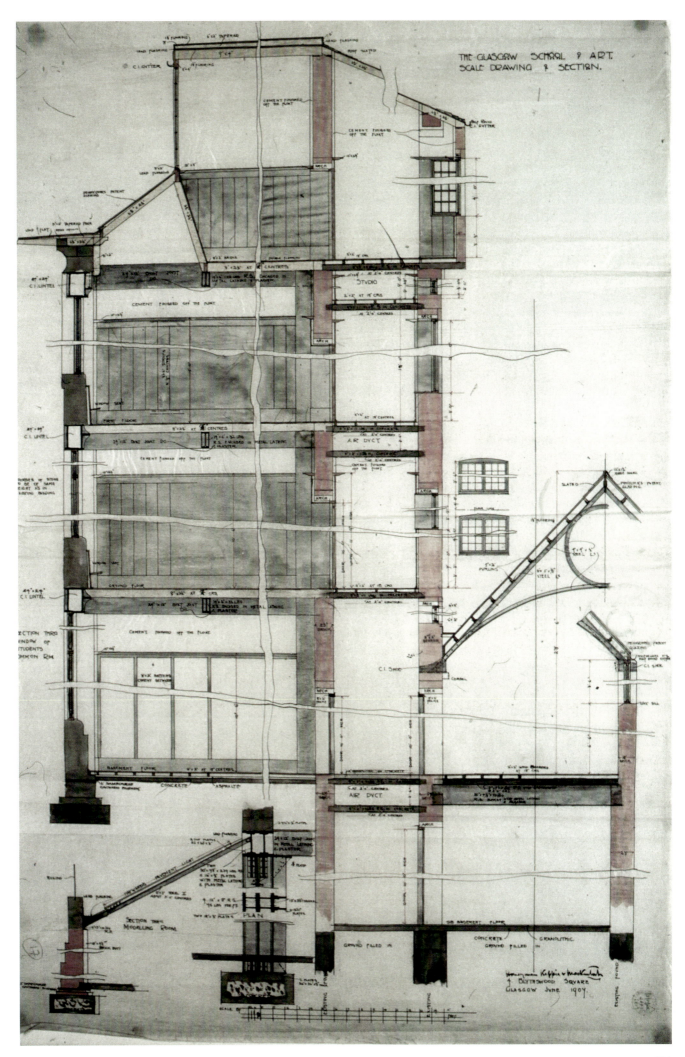

Second Phase
1907–1909

第二期
1907〜1909

Overall Structure and Library

The overall structure consists of an E-shaped plan, featuring a gallery in the center with a glass roof and skylight, a library and workshop on the 2 sides, and studios on the second and third floors on the north side. Large iron-framed windows were installed to achieve uniform lighting throughout the studio which was an important requirement of the competition. To suppress vibrations passing through the building, the windows are supported by a wrough-iron truss structure in the form of floral ornaments.

In the second phase, an additional layer was added to the top floor and the pitched roof of the studio in the original plan was removed, thereby reconfiguring it as a flat-roofed building, an embodiment of modern architecture.

The overall structure of the building itself consists of masonry on the exterior, steel for the beams, concrete for the floors, and steel for the reinforcement of large openings – a hybrid combination achieved by using the right materials in the appropriate places. Inside, the interior is a surprisingly wooden space that makes liberal use of this material. The building was fully equipped with an air-conditioning system for the whole building, elevators, and electric lighting, which were still state-of-the-art at the time. In contrast, the top floor features closed corridors with alcoves in a massive, bolted basement-like structure. Here, the doors open into a glass greenhouse called the Henllan (birdhouse), an observation deck with views of the city of Glasgow.

The library is the most important space of the building and a fine demonstration of Mackintosh's design competence and a showcase for his originality. It consists of 3 levels, with a double-height atrium in the center, a book gallery along the perimeter, and stacks for books on the floor above. In the library, the latticework ceiling is connected to the wooden floor structure of the stacks, the latter of which is a suspended structure reinforced with twisted iron rods.

The interior space was probably the first of its kind in England or on the continent to be so delicately and superbly constructed of wood at the time. The external sash windows and internal doors are designed with a similar grid motif that is connected to all the light fixtures, furniture, interior, and building elements, creating a sacred space of art that is conceived as a totality.

全体構成とライブラリー

全体の構成は、E型プランに纏められ、ガラス屋根のトップライトのある中央にギャラリー、両サイドに図書室とアトリエ、北面には、2層と3層のスタジオを配している。コンペの重要な要件であったスタジオの均一採光の為に、鉄の窓梁による大開口部の窓と、この大窓の鉄の花装飾に見える窓振動を抑えるトラス構造を設けている。

第二期では、オリジナル案から、最上階に1層分の増築を行い、元のスタジオの勾配屋根をとり払い、近代建築の様相であるフラットルーフの建築へと全体を再構成している。

建築構造は、外観は石造、梁は鉄骨造、床はコンクリート造、大開口部の補強に鉄材を使用し、適材適所に混合させたハイブリッドに全体が構成された建築である。中に入ると木を多用した木造のような意外性のある空間が展開する。そして当時、まだ最新であった全館空調システムやエレヴェータ、電気照明の設備が完備されていた。最上階には、対照的に、地階のようなマッシヴなヴォールト構造のアルコーヴのある閉ざされた廊下と、ドアを開けるとガラス温室のヘンラン（鳥小屋）と呼ばれる展望台があり、グラスゴーの街並みを眺望できる。

ライブラリーは、この建築の最重要空間であり、マッキントッシュのデザイン力を示し、そのオリジナリティが発揮された空間である。中央部に2層吹き抜けと周辺に書籍のギャラリーが配され、上階の書庫からなる3層空間である。ライブラリーの格子組天井は、書庫の木床構造になり、この床は捻れ鉄棒で補強された吊り構造である。

恐らく当時、木造によってこれ程繊細で卓越したインテリア空間は、英国内、大陸でも類を見なかったであろう。外部サッシと内部のドアが同じような格子モチーフでデザインされ、このグリッド・モチーフは、照明・家具・インテリア・建物エレメントのすべてを連動させ、トータルに創造された神聖な芸術空間をつくりだしている。

Opposite: Exterior view of the bay window in the double-height atrium of the library. The library was redesigned during the expansion of the west wing in the second phase. The west façade has a neat geometric design with a series of vertical bay windows, while the south has a simple rustic finish with vertical sunken windows, thus creating a solid-void relationship.

右頁：吹き抜けの図書室出窓、外観。第二工期の西棟増築では、図書室などが再デザインされた。西面が連奏する縦長出窓の端正な幾何学的デザインであるのにたいし、南面には素朴なラスカスト仕上げの窪んだ縦長窓が配され、ネガポジのデザインとなっている。

This page: West entrance. In contrast to the art nouveau design of the first phase, the second phase reveals a shift toward art deco with the use of geometric abstraction in the motifs which depict natural elements, such as layered clouds and raindrops. Opposite: Close-up of the solid-void contrast between the west and south façade.

本頁：西側の入口。第一工期のアール・ヌーヴォー的デザインにたいし、第二工期では重層する雲や雨滴など自然をモチーフとする幾何学的抽象に変化し、アール・デコに移行している。右頁：ネガポジのデザインがされた西と南の立面を見る。

145

p. 144: Staircase. p. 145, top: Boardroom, renovated in 1906. p. 145, bottom: Attic studio. Opposite: Painting studio with a large double-height window. To provide uniform lighting, Mackintosh installed large windows on the building's north wall. The lintel and sash of the window opening are reinforced with steel, and supported by wrought-iron brackets visible outside the window. This page, top: Close-up of the attic studio skylight. This page, bottom: Studio.

144頁：階段室。145頁、上：1906年に改修された理事会議室。145頁、下：アティック・スタジオ。左頁：吹抜けの大開口窓のある絵画スタジオ。スタジオに必要であった均一採光のためマッキントッシュは北面に大開口窓を設けている。開口上部のまぐさとサッシはスティールで補強され、サッシの揺れ留めに鉄装飾のトラスバットレスが設けられた。本頁、上：アティック・スタジオの天窓ディテール。本頁、下：スタジオ。

pp. 148–149: The double-height library has a corridor of books along the second floor and a wooden lattice ceiling suspended from the floor above by wrought-iron ties. This page, top: Hexagonal void, next to the vertical bay windows along the west, fills the library with natural daylight. This page, bottom: Bay windows. Opposite: View of the library from the second-floor corridor. Photo by Shinkenchiku-sha.

148〜149頁：図書室。3層で構成され、2階は回廊、3階は木造格子天井とスティール・バーで補強された吊り床構造の書庫。本頁、上：六角形のヴォイド。西側の縦長出窓に合わせ、書庫壁面に六角形のヴォイドを設けることで採光を確保している。本頁、下：出窓。右頁：2階ギャラリーから図書室を見る。

Essay:
More Conditions than Sentiments: Revealed by Fire
Sally Stewart

エッセイ：
感情よりも状況を：火災が明らかにしたもの
サリー・スチュワート
松本晴子訳

Through 2 fires, the first limited in its impact and the other catastrophic, the original fabric of Mackintosh's Glasgow School of Art (pp. 116–151) has been lost, although the memory and presence of the building remains palpable. It is small compensation therefore, to consider what has been discovered afresh about the building through this intrinsically destructive process. Nevertheless, new understanding and knowledge have resulted from the initial investigations and subsequent restoration processes following the 2014 Mackintosh fire, and likely to come with the future rebuilding necessitated by the catastrophic 2018 fire.

"In many other ways the Glasgow School of Art gives an illusion of practicality and a sturdy willingness to do its job."[1]

Well-tempered environment
Though based on the model typology of an art school developed by the Kensington and Chelsea Examination Board and deployed in several contemporary institutions, Glasgow School of Art benefited significantly from the alignment of program, context and technology. Some of the key spatial qualities and success of the teaching spaces resulted from the specific approach to orientation, and the exploitation of dualities of north-south, east-west condition. Critic Reyner Banham points out the original environmental conditioning of studio and other teaching spaces came from Charles Rennie Mackintosh's understanding of having to recognize – or more actively compensate for – the enormous areas of north-facing glass, and that this necessity is largely overlooked in favor of "new concepts of space."[2]

Perhaps the contribution of materials and construction is the least well documented aspect of the project, often mentioned only from a phenomenological viewpoint. Whatever the choice of materials, their predictability and behavior over time and in extreme circumstances reveal one of the most interesting aspects of the fires in 2014 and 2018.

Robustness
Load-bearing masonry and brick walls made up the bulk of the building's vertical structure, with steel and timber beams and joists tied within it. With the exception of steel, these are traditional local building materials – massive and stable, yet adaptable. Built in 2 phases, the building was constructed as 2 essentially separate structures with a shared wall to the west of the first phase. This aspect was critical in the first fire, separating the 2 sets of spaces and limiting the openings where fire could pass through.

二度にわたる火災——一度目の影響は限定的で二度目は壊滅的であった——により、マッキントッシュ設計のグラスゴー美術学校（116〜151頁）はオリジナルの建物構造を失ったが、建物の記憶と存在は今もまさにそこにある。したがって、きわめて破壊的であったプロセスを通じ新たに明らかになった事柄をもってしてもわずかな埋め合わせにしかならないだろう。しかし、2014年の火災後に行われた初期調査とその後の修復過程がもたらした新たな理解と知識は、2018年の壊滅的な火災によって必要となった将来の再建にとって不可欠のものとなるだろう。本論ではこうした知識について概説する。

「ほかの多くの点で、グラスゴー美術学校は、実用性の幻想とその仕事をするための不屈の意欲を与えてくれる」。[1]

うまく調節された環境
グラスゴー美術学校は、ケンジントン・アンド・チェルシー審査会による、現代的機関で展開されている美術学校モデルにもとづきつつも、プログラム・コンテクスト・テクノロジーの提携によって大きな恩恵を受けていた。重要である空間的性質と教育空間は、方位にたいするアプローチや、南北・東西条件の二重性の利用といった要因によってきわめて成功していた。批評家レイナー・バンハムは、スタジオやその他教育空間の元々の環境調整は、北向きの広大なガラス張りエリアの必要性をマッキントッシュが理解しており、このことは「新しい空間概念」に目がいくばかりでほとんど見過ごされてきたと指摘する。[2]

素材・構造については最小限しか文書化されておらず、現象学的な観点からのみ言及がされている場合が多い。とはいえ、素材の選択、経年変化、そして極状況下での変化は、2014、2018年の火災から明らかになった興味深い側面である。

堅牢性
耐荷重性の石積みと煉瓦壁が建物の縦構造大部分を構成しており、そこには鋼鉄・木材梁・根太が結びつけられていた。鋼鉄を除くと、地元の伝統的な建材であり、頑丈で安定しつつも改造可能である。二期で建てられたこの建物は、本質的に2つの別々の構造体として建設され、第一期建物の西側には共有の仕切り壁が存在した。2つの空間が分離されており、火炎を通す開口部が限定されていたことは、最初の火災において重要であった。

建設段階にあった数年の間にグラスゴーの建築基準規制付則が、この工業都市全体で多く発生していた工場施設の故障、とりわけ火災に対応し、変更された。この規制にしたがって、第二期では防火のために3階部分に仕上げコンクリートが導入された。こうして耐火性能の高い堅牢な床が効率的に設置された。2度目の火災時に内部の仕切り壁と床がすべて破損した後でも、石積みの壁の剛性が効果的に増したことはさらに重要であった。火災が生みだした熱と動的影響に耐えた

In the years between the building phases Building Regulations and by-laws in Glasgow had changed, developing in response to building failures, particularly numerous fires, in the factories across the industrial city. A concrete screed was thus needed at the second-floor level for fire separation across the whole building during the completion of the later phase, efficiently providing a robust fireproof floor, but more importantly, effectively increasing the rigidity of the masonry walls during the second fire after all other internal partitions and floors failed. Arguably, it was this screed that saved the structure from the intensity and dynamic impact of the fire's heat.

Other equally simple and mundane building techniques and materials limited the impact of the 2014 fire. In the days immediately after the fire, when the building's contents were moved to safety by teams of staff volunteers, it became clear that enlarged timber checks around fire doors had limited the fire's spread for much longer than expected. Doors in the west staircase showed charring on one side, making the ferocity of the fire palpable.

Also, the original Georgian wired glass, a glass cast with a wide wire mesh in its thickness and used in situations where fire protection is needed throughout the building, performed as designed; skylights, fanlights and screens remained intact, structurally sound against the fire.

Although stonework had been exposed to intense heat, even during the 2014 fire, the comparison of detailed digital surveys carried out before and after the fire allowed the extent of damage to be studied within key areas, such as the library's south and west façades (which was deemed minimally damaged), and the risk of failure to be calculated. The extent of stonework to be replaced was subsequently minimized through X-ray technology.

The intensity of the 2018 fire stripped all remaining surfaces back to their original state, with the brickwork in particular unscathed while plaster and other finishes failed. What is remarkable is the predictability of basic, commonly used materials to resist fire as intended, materials that have been used locally for centuries and are still in regular use today.

The Dilemma of Restoration versus Conservation

Following the 2014 fire it became apparent how much information there was available about Glasgow School of Art, through detailed measured surveys, historical and contemporary photographic records, digital surveys and modeling, to name a few. While major damage was limited to a key spaces to the west, around the library, the room was used for a postgraduate studio and lecture theater, substantial amounts of the building suffered little or no damage. Questions regarding what to do, whether to restore the building exactly to the original, or to conserve traces of the fire's impact, were raised. Closest possible restoration to the original building became the team's objective.

The damage of the 2018 fire has raised different questions. To what extent can a modern facsimile take the place of the original? It is as much a cultural dilemma as an architectural and constructional one. While we reconcile ourselves to the lengthy rebuilding process, the memory and presence of the original must sustain us – a situation I think Mackintosh would have appreciated.

Notes:
1. Robert Harbison, *Masters of Building: Glasgow School of Art, The Architects Journal 24*, no. 189 (June 14,1989), p. 51.
2. Reyner Banham, *The Architecture of the Well-Tempered Environment* (London: The Architectural Press, 1969), pp. 84–86.

Sally Stewart is the head of Mackintosh School of Architecture, at Glasgow School of Art. She graduated with Bachelor of Architecture (Hons) and Master of Architecture from Mackintosh School of Architecture. Prior to her teaching career, she practiced as a licensed architect working on projects that involved regeneration, preservation, adaptive reuse, and the community.

構造へ私たちは感謝しなければならない。

同様に、2014年の火災の影響を限定的なものにしたのも、シンプルでありふれた建築技術・建材であった。防火扉周辺の拡大された木製の押さえ具は、期待されていた時間をはるかに超えて延焼を十分に制限したことがわかっている。これは、火災直後の数日間、スタッフらによるボランティアが内部に残されたものを安全な場所に移動した際に明らかとなった。西側階段の扉の片側は黒焦げになっており、火炎の激しさを感じさせた。

さらに、元々のジョージ王朝様式金網入りガラスは厚みのある金網を用いた鋳造ガラスであり、建物全体で防火が必要な場所に使用されていた。これは設計通りに機能し、天窓・扇型窓・スクリーンなどは損傷を免れており、構造的に安定しつつも延焼を止めたことがわかっている。

2014年の火災時でさえ石積みは炎熱にさらされたが、火災の前後に実施された詳細なデジタル調査を比較すると、図書館の南側と西側のファサードなど重要箇所での移動範囲を特定でき、倒壊のリスクが計算された。X線によって石積みを交換する範囲は最小限に抑えられた。

2018年の火災は非常に激しく、残されていた表面はすべて焼け落ち素材本来の状態に戻り、煉瓦構造自体は無傷であったが漆喰やその他仕上げは失われた。注目に値するのは、何世紀にもわたって地元で一般に使用され、今日でも通常使用されている基本素材が意図通りに耐火性を発揮していたという予測可能性である。

修復と保存のジレンマ

2014年の火災後、詳細な測定調査、記録写真、近年の写真記録、デジタル調査、モデリングなどを通し、グラスゴー美術学校について入手可能な情報がどれだけあるかが明らかになった。大きな被害は西側の図書館、作曲室、現大学院スタジオ、講義室の周りなど、主要な空間に限定され、建物の大部分はほとんど／まったく被害を受けていなかった。次にやるべきこと——オリジナルを完全かつ直接的に復原するか、もしくは火災の痕跡をなんらかのかたちで保存するか——が問われていた。当時決定されたのは、オリジナルの状態に可能な限り戻すということであった。

2018年の火災による壊滅的影響は様々な疑問を投げかけた。近代的複写はどこまでオリジナルの建物にとって代わることができるか。これは文化的ジレンマであると同時に、建築的・構造的なジレンマでもある。我々は長きにわたる再建築のプロセスを甘受する一方で、当初の建物の記憶と存在に支えられている。これにはマッキントッシュも喜んでくれるだろうか。

原註：
1. 英文参照
2. 邦訳はレイナー・バンハム、堀江悟郎訳『環境としての建築　建築デザインと環境技術』（SD選書、鹿島出版会、2013、pp. 84–86）

p. 147, top left: Emergency services putting out the fire at the Glasgow School of Art, 2018. Photos on pp. 147 courtesy of Sally Stewart. p. 147, top right: Corridor after the fire in 2014. p. 147, bottom left: Scaffolding supporting the exterior walls before renovation. p. 147, middle: View from the top floor after the fire in 2014. p.147, bottom right: The brick masonry exposed after the wooden interior was destroyed by the fire in 2014.

147頁、左上：2018、グラスゴー美術学校の火災を消し止める救急隊。147頁、右上：2014年の火災後の廊下。147頁、左下：改修前の外壁を支える足場。147頁、中：2014年の火災後、最上階からの眺め。147頁、右下：2014年に起きた火災で木造の内装が焼失し、露出した煉瓦組み。

サリー・スチュワートは、グラスゴー芸術大学マッキントッシュ建築学校校長。マッキントッシュ建築学校で学び、建築学士号（優等学位）および建築学修士号を取得。建築家としての資格を取得後、建築家として再生・保存・再利用・コミュニティにかかわるプロジェクトにたずさわり、その後教育活動を開始している。

Glasgow Herald
Glasgow, United Kingdom 1895

グラスゴー・ヘラルド
英国、グラスゴー　1895

Glasgow Herald is the head office for the newspaper publishing company in the city of Glasgow. Standing at the beginning of Mitchell Street, which runs along a north-south axis in the heart of the city near the central train station, the building, with its tower, gives a strong presence. Charles Rennie Mackintosh's perspective drawing of Glasgow Herald in art nouveau style appeared in the February 1895 issue of the architectural magazine *British Architect*, which described it as "a notable new building in Glasgow."

During his 1891 trip to Italy on the Alexander Thompson travel scholarship, Mackintosh became fascinated by the bell towers he saw, and he made numerous sketches of these structures in his Italian sketchbook. After returning to Glasgow, this strong inspiration led him to propose twin tower designs for the Glasgow Art Gallery (1891–1892) and Railway Terminus (1892–1893) competitions. Mackintosh also made 3 primary sketches of his ideas for the tower of the Herald Building on the last blank page of his Italian sketchbook. Today, Glasgow Herald has been expanded and is being used as The Lighthouse, a tourist information facility for the city of Glasgow.

Translated by Darryl Jingwen Wee

グラスゴー・ヘラルドは、グラスゴーの新聞社本社屋であり、市内中心地、中央駅近くの南北軸に伸びるミッチェル通りの起点に建っている。塔のあるグラスゴー・ヘラルド・ビルが存在感を示している。マッキントッシュが描いたアール・ヌーヴォー・タッチのパースペクティヴ図は、建築雑誌『British Architect』1895年2月号に掲載され、グラスゴーの注目すべき新建築と紹介されている。

マッキントッシュは、1891年のアレキサンダー・トムソン・トラベル奨学金によるイタリア旅行の際、鐘塔に強く心打たれようで、彼のイタリアン・スケッチブックには、塔のスケッチが多数描かれている。帰国後、その強いインスピレーションは、グラスゴー・アート・ギャラリー案（1891～1892）および鉄道終着駅案（1892～1893）の双頭塔のアイディアのコンペ案として提案された。また、マッキントッシュは、グラスゴー・ヘラルド・ビルの塔のアイディアを、イタリアン・スケッチブックの最後の空白ページに、3つのプライマリー・スケッチとして描いている。現在、グラスゴー・ヘラルドの建物は、グラスゴー市の観光案内施設のライト・ハウスとして増改築され、使われている。

This page, top: Exterior. The presence of the symbolic and distinctive building and its tower can be felt from afar. Photo courtesy of Hiroaki Kimura. Opposite: Perspective sketch of the building along Mitchell Street. Sketch courtesy of The Hunterian, University of Glasgow.

本頁、上：外観。遠くからでもその存在を感じられるシンボリックで特徴的な塔。右頁：ミッチェル通りからのパースペクティヴ。

Queen's Cross Church
Glasgow, United Kingdom 1896–1899

クイーンズ・クロス教会
英国、グラスゴー　1896〜1899

The commission for Queen's Cross Church came from the Free Church of Saint Matthew in Springbank, one of 12 churches built in Glasgow's newer neighborhoods. It is located on Maryhill Road, which stretches to the north of the city of Glasgow, in an area of tenement complexes.

Design began in early 1897; the foundation stone was installed on June 23, 1898; the first service was held on September 10, 1899; and the Dean of Guild (D&G) records that construction was completed on May 17, 1900.

Church architecture was a major body of work for Charles Rennie Mackintosh, including Queen's Cross Church, Ruchill Free Church Halls (1899), and the Liverpool Cathedral competition (1901–1902). He carried a sketchbook with him at all times, drew many churches, and made detailed sketches of those that gave him inspiration. In particular, his sketches of the façade and octagonal tower of Church of All Saints in Merriott, Somerset, are directly reflected in the façade of Queen's Cross Church.

Mackintosh designed this church in 1897, during the most important period of his career. The year before he had submitted his winning design in the competition for the new Glasgow School of Art (pp. 116–151), which marked the dawn of modern architecture. During this time he also worked on many other projects, including the interiors and furniture for Miss Cranston's Tea Rooms (pp. 92–109), demonstrating his prominence in the world of architecture.

Mackintosh had been experimenting with a peculiar architectural style, a free idiom of art nouveau curves and ornamentation that was not confined to the conventional church style. Mackintosh's imagination is reflected in his delicate art nouveau style perspective drawings of this church which depicts an unfinished architecture of what appears to be an art school building and apartment complex behind it. The name of the church is noted as the Free Church of Saint Matthew.

Today, Queen's Cross Church is preserved and used as the headquarters of the Charles Rennie Mackintosh Society, the organization dedicated to the preservation of Mackintosh's architecture.

Translated by Darryl Jingwen Wee

pp. 160–161: Mackintosh's perspective drawing accurately depicts the architecture itself at the eye level. Behind the church is a building reminiscent of Glasgow School of Art and an apartment complex in Mackintosh style. Sketch courtesy of The Hunterian, University of Glasgow. This page, top: Façade along Garscube Road. Photos on pp. 162–163 courtesy of Hiroaki Kimura. This page, middle: View of the pulpit from a balcony on the second floor. Opposite: Close-ups of the art nouveau curves and mystical decoration details.

160～161頁：マッキントッシュのパースペクティヴ図はアイ・レヴェルで建築自体を正確に描いている。建物の背後にはグラスゴー美術学校を思わせる建物とマッキントッシュ風デザインの集合住宅が見える。
本頁、上：ガースキューブ通りからの外観。
本頁、中：2階バルコニーより説教台を見る。
右頁：アール・ヌーヴォー風の曲線とミスティズムな装飾。

クイーンズ・クロス教会は、スプリングバンク・ミッションのセント・マシュー・フリー・チャーチから依頼され、グラスゴーの新地区の12の教会の一つとして建てられた。グラスゴー市内の北部に伸びるメルヒル通りの、テーネメント群が建つ地域である。
1897年のはじめに設計が始まり、礎石は1898年6月23日に設置され、最初の礼拝は1899年9月10日に行われ、ディーン・オブ・ギルドには、1900年5月17日建築完了の記録がある。

マッキントッシュにとって教会建築は主要な作品であり、クイーンズ・クロス教会を始め、ロッヒル・ストリートの教会、リバプール・カテドラルのコンペ計画案等がある。彼は、常にスケッチブックをもち歩き、インスピレーションとなる教会やその詳細スケッチを多く描き残している。特に、サマーセットシャー、メリオットのオール・セインツ教団のための小さな教会を描いた、正面立面と八角塔のスケッチは、そのままクイーンズ・クロス教会の正面ファサードに反映されている。

この教会を設計する1897年頃は、近代建築の夜明けとなるグラスゴー美術学校新校舎（116～151頁）の設計コンペを勝ちとり、また、クランストン夫人のティールーム（92～109頁）のインテリア、家具等、多くの作品を同時に手掛け、建築界にその頭角を示した最も重要な時代である。
これまでの教会様式に囚われない、アール・ヌーヴォー的曲線と装飾のフリー・スタイルの特異な建築様式を試みていた。マッキントッシュが描いたこの教会の繊細なアール・ヌーヴォー・タッチの透視図には、そ

の背後にまだ完成していない美術学校らしき建築、そして恐らく集合住宅が描かれ、合わさってマッキントッシュの世界が描かれている。ここで教会名はセント・マシュー・フリー・チャーチと記されている。
現在、クイーンズ・クロス教会は、マッキントッシュ建築の保存団体であるマッキントッシュ・ソサエティーの本部として使用保存がされている。

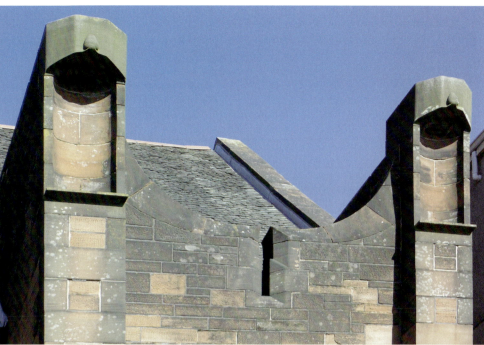

Scotland Street School
Glasgow, United Kingdom 1903–1907

スコットランド・ストリート・スクール
英国、グラスゴー　1903〜1907

On June 22, 1903, the School Board of Glasgow held its first meeting about this project; Charles Rennie Mackintosh submitted his first draft plan for it the following November; and the Dean of Guild (D&G) issued architectural approval a year later, on November 24, 1904. Finally, on October 6, 1906, the school officially opened, and today the building still stands directly in front of a station on the circular loop subway line. The overall architecture of this school is symmetrical and geometric. It uses a central corridor system, with 3 floors, extensive east-west length, and classrooms oriented toward the north and south.

Although this is a coeducational primary school, 2 symbolic towers of stairwells serve as separate entrances for boys and girls. The semicircular stairwells that form this distinctive feature are the 3-storey structures that resemble curtain walls reinforced with steel bars, an attempt to maximize openings for light to enter, and for transparency.

While the exterior walls are made of red sandstone, a material local to Glasgow, the interior of the hall is based on white tiles with extensive use of green tiles as a decorative accent. Otto Wagner of the Vienna School, with whom Mackintosh had a close friendship, made similarly liberal use of tile decoration during the same period. Following the beginning of the construction of Scotland Street School, work also began on the additional design of a small house for the guards. The juxtaposition of this public building with a contrasting small house at the corner of the site seems to demonstrate a certain equality among buildings of different scales. Mackintosh also designed The Hill House (pp. 12–49), together with a small guard house that is connected to the boundary wall, as if to contrast the large and small dwellings.

Translated by Darryl Jingwen Wee

pp. 164–165: Perspective drawing of Scotland Street School. Drawing courtesy of The Hunterian, University of Glasgow. Opposite, top: Front façade. The conical-roofed stair towers serve as separate entrances for girls and boys. Photos on pp. 165–167 courtesy of Hiroaki Kimura. Opposite, bottom: The north façade has a simple design with only the center bay accentuated by decorations. This page, top: Drill hall, 1916. This page, middle: Cookery classroom, 1916. This page, bottom: Ground-floor plan. Drawing courtesy of Glasgow City Archives.

学校委員会との最初の会議が行われたのは1903年6月22日であり、1903年11月に計画案が提出され、翌年11月24日にディーン・オブ・ギルドの建築承認が下り、1906年10月6日に正式に開校している。当時既に開通していた環状線地下鉄駅前の真正面に現在も建っている。建築全体は、シンメトリー的で、幾何学性が増し、3階建、東西に長く、教室群は中廊下方式による南北面に向けて計画されている。

男女共学のプライマリー・スクールであるが、入口は男女別々に分かれ、2つの象徴的なタワー状の階段室がその入校口である。特色をなす半円形の階段室は、3層に吹き抜け、カーテンウォールのように鉄棒で補強がされた、光をとり込む最大限の開口による透明感のあるデザインを試みている。

外壁には、グラスゴーの地産石材である赤左岸を使い、ホール内部には、白タイルを基調に、緑タイルの装飾を多用している。当時親交のあったウィーン派のオットー・ワーグナーも同様に同時期にタイル装飾を多用していた。また、スコットランド・ストリート・スクールの建設が始まり、その後に、守衛の為の小住宅を追加デザインとして行っている。敷地内隅に対照的な守衛の小住宅を設け、公共建築と大小の建築における平等性を示すかのように併設させている。マッキントッシュは、これまでも大小の住宅を対照させるかのように、ヒル・ハウス（12～49頁）と外構壁に連続する守衛の為の小住宅をあわせてデザインを行っている。

164～165頁：スコットランド・ストリート・スクールのパースペクティヴ図。左頁、上：正面、円錐形の屋根をもつ階段塔は、女子と男子別の入口として機能している。左頁、下：北ファサード、中央のベイだけが装飾で強調されたシンプルなファサード。本頁、上：ドリル・ホール（1916）。本頁、中央：調理室（1916）。本頁、下：地上階平面図。

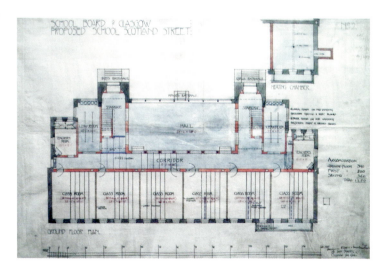

This page, top: Looking up the stair tower. This page, bottom left: Bright white and green tiles, with green-painted iron balusters that trace along the staircase. This page, bottom right: The dark colored door and floor contrast with the white-tiled wall. Opposite: Stair tower. The landings act like interior balconies that overlook the uninterrupted vertical space.

本頁、上：階段室を見上げる。本頁、左下：白と緑の鮮やかなタイルと緑に塗られた鉄製の手摺子が直線的な階段に沿って続いている。本頁、右下：濃い色の木と床、白いタイルの壁とのコントラスト。右頁：階段塔。踊り場は遮るもののない垂直な空間を眺めるインテリア・バルコニーのような役割を果たす。

Project List

プロジェクト・リスト

1888	Town House in a Terrace (student design)	高台のテラス・ハウス（学内デザイン）
1888	Mountain Chapel (student design)	マウンテン・チャペル（学内デザイン）
1888–1889	Wylie Hill's Store, Glasgow (built, for John Hutchison Architects, fig. 1)	ワイリー・ヒル店舗、ブキャナン通り、グラスゴー（実作、ジョン・ハッチソン・アーキテクツ、図1）
1889	Presbyterian Church (student design)	長老派教会（学内デザイン）
1890	Science and Art Museum (student design)	科学芸術博物館（学内デザイン）
1890	Public Hall (competition, Alexander Thomson Travelling Scholarship, fig. 3)	公共ホール（コンペ案、アレクサンダー・トムソン・トラベリング奨学金、図3）
1890	140–142 Balgrayhill Road (originally known as Redclyffe and Torrisdale), Glasgow (built, fig. 2)	バルグレイヒル通り140～142（レッドクリフ邸とトリスデイル邸）、グラスゴー、（実作、図2）
1890–1891	Workmen's Dwellings, Glasgow (competition)	労働者住居、グラスゴー、ロッテンロー＆ハイ・ストリート（コンペ案）
1891	Chapter House (competition)	チャプター・ハウス（コンペ案）
1891–1892	Glasgow Art Galleries (competition, for Honeyman & Keppie, fig. 4)	グラスゴー・アート・ギャラリー（コンペ案、ハニーマン＆ケペ、図4）
1891–1893	Canal Boatmen's Institute, Glasgow (built, for Honeyman & Keppie)	カナル・ボートマン協会、グラスゴー、ポート・ダンダス通り（実作、ハニーマン＆ケペ）
1892	Manchester Municipal Technical School (competition, for Honeyman & Keppie)	マンチェスター技術学校（コンペ案、ハニーマン＆ケペ）
1892–1893	Railway Terminus (competition, fig. 5)	鉄道終着駅（コンペ案、図5）
1892–1893	Additions and Alterations to Glasgow Art Club, Glasgow (built, for Honeyman & Keppie, fig. 7)	グラスゴー・アート・クラブ増築改修、グラスゴー、バス通り（実作、ハニーマン＆ケペ、図7）
1892–1897	Additions and Alterations to Craigie Hall, Glasgow (built, for Honeyman & Keppie)	クレイギー・ホール増築改修、グラスゴー、ローワン通り（実作、ハニーマン＆ケペ）
1892–1899	Glasgow Herald (pp. 156–157, for Honeyman & Keppie)	グラスゴー・ヘラルド（156～157頁、ハニーマン＆ケペ）
1894–1895	Queen Margaret College Anatomical Department, Glasgow (built, for Honeyman & Keppie)	クイーン・マーガレット医科大学解剖学部、グラスゴー、クイーン・マーガレット通り（実作、ハニーマン＆ケペ）
1895	Inn at Lennoxtown (design)	レノックスタウンの宿（計画案）
1895–1897	Martyrs Public School, Glasgow (built, for Honeyman & Keppie, fig. 8)	マータス・パブリック・スクール、グラスゴー、パーソン通り（実作、ハニーマン＆ケペ、図8）
1895–1896	Buchanan Street Tea Room (pp. 104–105, decorations and furnishings)	ブキャナン・ストリート・ティールーム（104～105頁、装飾と調度品）
1896–1906	Glasgow School of Art, first phase (pp. 116–151)	グラスゴー美術学校、第一期（116～151頁）
1896–1899	Queen's Cross Church, Glasgow (pp. 158–161)	クイーンズ・クロス教会、グラスゴー（158～161頁）
1897–1898	Argyle Street Tea Rooms, Glasgow (p. 106, interior)	アーガイル・ストリート・ティールーム、グラスゴー（106頁、内装）
1898	National Bank of Scotland, Glasgow (competition)	スコットランド国立銀行、グラスゴー（コンペ案）
1898	Glasgow International Exhibition 1901 (competition, for Honeyman & Keppie, fig. 6)	1901年グラスゴー国際博覧会（コンペ案、ハニーマン＆ケペ、図6）
1898	Bedroom and Bathroom for Westdel, 2 Queen's Place, Glasgow (built)	2クイーンズ・パレス、ウェストデルの寝室浴室、グラスゴー（実作）
1898	Dining Room for Hugo Bruckmann, Munich, Germany (built)	ヒューゴ・ブルックマン邸ダイニング、ドイツ、ミュンヘン（実作）
1898–1900	Additions and Alterations to 233 St Vincent Street, Glasgow (built, for oneyman & Keppie)	233セント・ヴィンセント通り増築改修、グラスゴー（実作、ハニーマン＆ケペ）

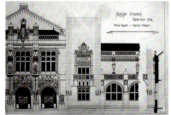

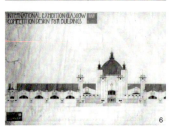
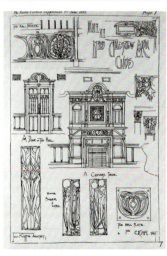

1899	Ruchill Free Church Halls, Glasgow (built, for Honeyman & Keppie)	ロッヒル・フリー・チャーチのホール、グラスゴー（実作、ハニーマン＆ケペ）
1899–1900	Additions and Alterations to Gourock Parish Church (built, for Honeyman & Keppie)	ゴウロック教区教会増築改修（実作、ハニーマン＆ケペ）
1899–1901	Windy Hill, Kilmacolm (pp. 58–65)	ウィンディ・ヒル、キルマコーム (58〜65頁)
1899–1900	Artist's House and Studio in the Country (p. 73)	芸術家の田園住宅兼スタジオ (73頁)
1899–1900	Artist's Town House (p. 72)	芸術家の都市住宅 (72頁)
1900–1904	Daily Record Building, Glasgow (built, for Honeyman & Keppie, figs. 9, 10)	デイリー・レコード・ビルディング、グラスゴー（実作、ハニーマン＆ケペ、図9、10）
1900	Interiors for Dunglass Castle, Bowling (built)	ダングラス・キャッスルの内装、ボウリング（実作）
1900	Mackintosh House, 120 Mains Street, Glasgow (pp. 76–87)	マッキントッシュ自邸、120メインズ通り、グラスゴー (76〜87頁)
1900–1901	Ingram Street Tea Rooms, Glasgow (p. 107)	イングラム・ストリート・ティールーム、グラスゴー (107頁)
1900	Room Setting for the 8th Exhibition of the Vienna Secession, Austria (built)	第8回ウィーン分離派展、展示デザイン、オーストリア（実作）
1900–1901	Stand for Glasgow School of Art, 1901 Glasgow International Exhibition (built)	グラスゴー美術学校ブース、1901年グラスゴー国際博覧会（実作）
1901	House for an Art Lover (fig. 11, pp. 66–71)	芸術愛好家の家（図11、66〜71頁）
1901	Bathroom addition to 29 Hamilton Drive, Glasgow (built, for Honeyman & Keppie)	29ハミルトン・ドライヴ浴室増築（実作）
1901	Stencilled decoration, St. Serf's Church, Dysart (built)	ステンシル装飾、セント・サーフズ・チャーチ、ディザート（実作）
1901	Golf Club House (plan)	ゴルフ・クラブ・ハウス（計画案）
1901	Interiors for 14 Kingsborough Gardens, Glasgow (built)	14キングスボロウガーデン内装、グラスゴー（実作）
1901–1902	Auchenbothie Gate Lodge, Kilmacolm (pp. 74–75)	オーチェンボシー邸、ゲート・ロッジ、キルマコーム (74〜75頁)
1901–1902	Liverpool Cathedral (competition, fig. 14)	リバプール大聖堂（コンペ案、図13）
1902	House at Kilmacolm (design)	キルマコームの家（計画）
1902	Headington, Bridge of Weir (built, figs. 12, 13, drawings are signed by Keppie)	ヘディントン邸、ブリッジ・オブ・ワイル（実作、図12、15、図面にはケペの署名あり）
1902	Scottish Section for the International Exhibition of Modern Decorative Art, Turin, Italy (built, fig. 15)	トリノ現代装飾美術国際展示会、スコットランド部門、イタリア（実作、図14）
1902	Music Salon for Fritz Waerndorfer (built)	フリッツ・ヴェルンドルファー邸音楽サロン（実作）
1902	Room Setting for the Architecture and Craft of the New Style Exhibition, Moscow (built, fig. 16)	モスクワ建築工芸新様式展示会、室内装飾展示（実作、図16）
1902–1904	The Hill House, Helensburgh (pp. 12–49)	ヒル・ハウス、ヘレンズバラ (12〜49頁)
1902–1904	Willow Tea Rooms, Glasgow (pp. 92–103)	ウィロー・ティールーム、グラスゴー 92〜103頁
1903	Bedroom for the Dresdener Werkstätte Exhibition, Germany (built)	ドレスデン工房展、寝室内装展示、ドイツ（実作）

169

1903–1905	Shop, Flat, and Offices, Comrie (built, fig. 17)	店舗兼アパート兼事務所、コムリー（実作、図17）	
1903–1907	Scotland Street School, Glasgow (pp. 162–167)	スコットランド・ストリート・スクール、グラスゴー（162～167頁）	
1903–1904	Chancel Furnishings, Bridge of Allan Parish Church (built)	ブリッジ・オブ・アラン教区教会、聖堂家具（実作）	
1904–1910	Hous'hill, Glasgow (pp. 88–91)	ハウス・ヒル、グラスゴー（88～91頁）	
1904–1905	Alterations to Ardarroch, Finnart (built)	アーダーロッホ邸改修、フィナート（実作）	
1904–1905	Alterations at 229–233 Sauchiehall Street, Glasgow (built)	ソキホール通り229～233改修、グラスゴー（実作）	
1905	Dining Room for the A. S. Ball Exhibition of Modern Furniture, Berlin, Germany (built)	A・S・ボール現代家具展、ダイニング展示、ドイツ、ベルリン（実作）	
1905–1906	Alterations to Abbey Close United Free Church, Paisley (built)	アビー・クロス・ユナイテッド・フリー・チャーチ改修、ペイズリー（実作）	
1905–1906	Dutch Kitchen, Addition to Argyle Street Tea Rooms, Glasgow (built)	ダッチ・キッチン、アーガイル・ストリート・ティールーム増築、グラスゴー（実作）	
1906	Lavatory and Kitchen, Addition to Willow Tea Room, Glasgow (built)	洗面所とキッチン、ウィロー・ティールーム増築、グラスゴー（実作）	
1906	Mackintosh House, 6 Florentine Terrace, Glasgow (pp. 76–87)	マッキントッシュ自邸、6フロレンティン・テラス、グラスゴー（76～87頁）	
1906	Additions and Alterations to 9 Grosvenor Terrace, Glasgow (design)	9グローヴナー・テラス増築改修、グラスゴー（計画案）	
1906	Exhibition Stand for Wilkinson Heywood & Clark Ltd. (design)	ウィルキンソン・ヘイウッド・アンド・クラーク社の展示台（計画案）	
1906–1907	Oak Room, Addition to Ingram Street Tea Rooms, Glasgow (built)	オーク・ルーム、イングラム・ストリート・ティールーム増築、グラスゴー（実作）	
1906–1908	Auchinibert, Killearn (built, figs. 18, 20)	オーチニベルト邸、キルアーン（実作、図18、20）	
1906–1907	Alterations to St Philip's United Free Church, Portobello (built)	セント・フィリップ・ユナイテッド・フリー・チャーチ改修、ポートベロー、エディンバラ（実作）	
1906–1907	Mossyde, First Phase (Ploughman's Cottage), Kilmacolm	モッサイド邸、第一期（農夫のコテージ、キルマコーム	
1907–1908	Addition to The Moss, Dumgoyne (built)	ザ・モス増築、ダムゴイン（実作）	
1907–1910	Glasgow School of Art, Second phase (pp. 116–151)	グラスゴー美術学校、第二期（116～151頁）	
1908–1910	Mossyde, Second Phase (Cottage at Cloak), Kilmacolm (built)	モッサイド邸、第二期（クロークのコテージ）、キルマコーム（実作）	
1908	Alterations to the Lady Artists' Club, Glasgow (built, fig. 22)	レディ・アーティスト・クラブ改修、グラスゴー（実作、図22）	
1909–1910	Oval Room and Ladies' Rest Room, Additions to Ingram Street Tea Rooms, Glasgow (built)	オーヴァル・ルームと女性用化粧室、イングラム・ストリート・ティールーム増築、グラスゴー（実作）	
1911–1912	Redesign of Cloister Room and Chinese Room, Ingram Street Tea Rooms, Glasgow (built)	クロイスター・ルームとチャイニーズ・ルーム改修、イングラム・ストリート・ティールーム、グラスゴー（実作）	
1911	White Cockade Café at Scottish National Exhibition, Glasgow (built, fig. 21)	ホワイト・コケイド・カフェ、スコットランド博覧会、グラスゴー（実作、図21）	
1911–1913	Additions to Auchenbothie, Kilmacolm (built, fig. 19)	オーチェンボシー邸増築、キルマコーム（実作、図19）	
1912	Alterations to Hairdressing Salon, Glasgow (design)	ヘアサロンの改修、グラスゴー（計画案）	

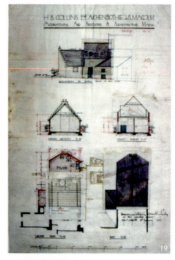

1913–1915	Mossyde, Third Phase, Kilmacolm (built, figs. 23, 25)	モッサイド邸、第三期、キルマコーム（実作、図23、25）
1916–1917	The Dug-Out, Addition to Willow Tea Rooms, Glasgow (pp. 102–103)	ダグアウト、ウィロー・ティールーム増築、グラスゴー（102～103頁）
1917–1920	78 Derngate, Northampton (pp. 110–115)	78ダンゲート、ノーサンプトン（110～115頁）
1917	Bedroom for Sidney Horstmann, Bath (built)	シドニー・ホーストマン邸寝室、バース（実作）
1918–1919	Alteration to Candida Cottage, Roade (built)	キャンディダ・コテージ改修、ロアード（実作）
1919–1920	Alterations to House at Little Hedgecourt, East Grinstead (design)	リトル・ヘッジコートの家改修、イースト・グリンステッド（計画案）
1920	Alterations to Studio for Alexander Stuart-Hill, London (built, fig. 24)	アレクサンダー・スチュアート・ヒルのスタジオ改修、ロンドン（実作、図24）
1920–1921	Addition and Alterations to Leigh Farm Cottages, Ansty (built)	リー・ファーム・コテージ増築改修、アンスティ（実作）
1920	Block of Studios and Studio-Flats for the Arts League of Service, London (design, fig. 26)	アーツ・リーグ・オブ・サービスのためのスタジオ・ブロックとスタジオ・フラット、ロンドン（計画案、図26）
1920	Studio-House for Arthur Cadogan Blunt, London (design)	アーサー・カドガン・ブラントのためのスタジオ・ハウス、ロンドン（計画案）
1920–1921	Studio-House for Harold Squire, London (built)	ハロルド・スクワイアのためのスタジオ・ハウス、ロンドン（実作）
1920	Building Containing Studios for Francis Derwent Wood, London (design)	フランシス・ダーウェント・ウッドのためのスタジオを含む建物、ロンドン（計画案）
1920	Theater for Margaret Morris, London (design)	マーガレット・モリスのための劇場、ロンドン（計画案）

23

24

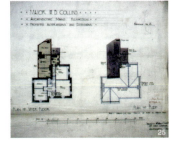 

25　26

Some Thoughts on Creative Collaboration

創造的協働への一考察

While some of Charles Rennie Mackintosh's works are readily identified by their singularity (watercolors, textile prints, botanic illustrations for example), much of his creative output derived from collaboration – some instances conventional and others more unorthodox in their form of exchange and impact. These are important to consider as they remind us of the range of ways architecture design is influenced and the behaviors architects and designers develop to support their creative practice, which was often underplayed or seen as incidental.

Newbery: Mentor
Mackintosh's relation to Francis Henry Newbery as tyro to mentor is documented. This dynamic took many forms, and the relationship evolved over the sustained period of their friendship; from Newbery's original recognition of skill and potential in a student, through drawing attention to and making available particular sources of inspiration such as *Iroha-biki moncho*, to supporting Mackintosh and his wife Margaret as a creative force and providing a model with his own wife Jessie of symbiotic partnership. Mackintosh and Newbery each recognized their own particular areas of interest and contributions, one as architect and the other as a leader in higher education, each complementing the other in their contributions to the conception and realization of the Glasgow School of Art building.

Margaret Macdonald Mackintosh: Life Partner
As a creative couple, the Mackintoshes were well matched, and this symmetry led to the development of individual that reenforced and reflected the other's thinking. Again, each played to their strengths, and rather than merging their ideas, they achieved diversity in the exploration of themes and narratives, each linked to and cognizant of the other. This intense, mature relationship was mutually supportive and created momentum – what we might now see as a safe space for experimentation, dreaming, and overlaps of roles and authorship. If we consider that the couple's respective art practices ran parallel with Mackintosh's professional career, we begin to recognize the intensity and extent of his continual immersion in design thinking.

The Four, Peers
If we think about the context of 2 sisters personally and creatively aligned to 2 best friends, the energy and dynamics of the Four, while they were students and afterward, emerges. As students they were insiders, seeing the workings of Glasgow School of Art firsthand, experiences that would have informed Mackintosh's perspective on what a new art school building should provide spatially and socially. Their shared values and thematic interests appear to have brought them together, with the tensions and difficulties they experienced individually coming from external forces and situations, rather than from within the group. They provided one another with a place for collaborative thinking and sympathetic discussion that few architects have access to, and it must have given confidence to Mackintosh as a young designer.

The following 3 collaborations, all underpinned with intimacy and trust, were 3 conventional situations within architectural practice, yet particularly notable as creative engines and collaborative opportunities in Mackintosh's body of work.

Honeyman and Keppie: Office
We now consider an architectural practice as a place of collaboration, and potential coauthorship. A building is seldom the labor of one person, and while we still may credit output to a group practice or even an individual creator, that is rarely an accurate depiction of the interactions involved in the realization of a work of architecture. Through the practice, we share resources, experience, and precedent. This is an active process rather than a passive one. The office of Honeyman and Keppie appears to accept that a single practice can pursue a variety of ideas stylistically while sharing authorship. Years of formal apprenticeship and evening classes at Glasgow School of Architecture had prepared Mackintosh for the orthodoxy of the professional practice he found at Honeyman and Keppie.[1] The experience of this practice also allowed Mackintosh to develop his design thinking radically over the period of hiatus in the completion of Glasgow School of Art, between its east and west façades, while still providing a continuous identity to the whole. That evolution evidenced a growing depth of design thinking rather than any change of mind.

Client: Patron and User
Mackintosh's connections and exchanges with his most important clients often extended beyond conventional distance and bounded roles to collaborative dialogues that were sustained, productive, and mutually respectful. As a result, and clear in the example of Glasgow School of Art, Mackintosh's agency and license increased, allowing him to pursue his preferred working methods and his designs to evolve in response to emerging situations, discoveries, and reflections. Here the client is transformed to patron with more to gain through the process of collaboration than through financial incentives.

In these creative collaborations, Mackintosh operated between spaces of orthodoxy and intimacy, and appears to have thrived in the heightened opportunities (and risks) this way of working provided. Mackintosh was influenced and in turn influenced others. The range of influences to be tapped into and his preparedness to respond to this input, leaving design open-ended to a very late stage of its development, was part of his *habitus* embedded in his personal and creative practice. While not unique to Mackintosh, it was fundamental to his work and its resulting synthesis is legible in the design of Glasgow School of Art and a contributing factor to its continuing relevance.

Sally Stewart

チャールズ・レニー・マッキントッシュの作品のうち、個人的制作物であると識別するのが容易なもの（水彩画、テキスタイルプリント、植物画など）がある一方、彼の職業人生において、その創作活動の多くが交流・影響による従来型の協働と型破りな協働の結果であったことは明白である。こうした協働のかたちは、建築設計が多岐にわたることで影響を受ける範囲と、建築家やデザイナーが創造的実践を支えるために身につける習性を考える上で重要となる。

ニューベリー：よき指導者
マッキントッシュとフランシス・ヘンリー・ニューベリーは初学者とよき指導者（メンター）の関係にあったことは記録されている。こうした関係は様々なかたちをとり、彼らの友情は長い期間にわたって発展した。ニューベリーは校長として、この学生に技量と可能性をはじめて認め、手元にあった『いろは引き紋章』など情報源に興味をもたせ、マッキントッシュとその妻マーガレットの創造的協働を支援し、彼自身の妻であるジェシーとの共生的パートナーシップのモデルを示した。マッキントッシュとニューベリーは自身の関心分野と貢献分野をそれぞれ認識しており、一方は建築家として、他方は指導者として、お互いがグラスゴー美術学校の建物構想とその実現に貢献した。

マーガレット・マクドナルド・マッキントッシュ：人生の伴侶
マッキントッシュ夫妻は協働をする夫婦としてぴったりであった。この釣り合いのとれた二人は個々の制作をさらに発展させ、お互いの考え方に影響を与え合っていた。ここでも二人はそれぞれの強みを生かして、アイディアを合体させるのではなく、テーマと物語の探求に多様性を与え、各自が互いにつながりながら認め合っていた。この強烈かつ成熟した関係は、相互に支え合うことで勢いを生みだしていた。現在の我々はそれを実験・夢・役割と作者が重なり合う安全な場所と見なすことができる。こうした背景がマッキントッシュの専門家キャリアと並行していたことを考慮するなら、彼がいかにデザインに絶えず没頭し、考え抜いていたか、その苛烈さが理解できるだろう。

ザ・フォーの仲間たち
2人の姉妹と、個人的かつ創造面で結ばれていた2人の親友らの関係を考えるにあたり、ザ・フォーがもっていたであろうエネルギーと激しさに思いがゆく。彼らは学生として、内部関係者としてグラスゴー美術学校の仕組みを直接体験しており、そうした経験は新しい美術学校校舎が空間的・社会的に何を提供すべきかについて、マッキントッシュにある見方を吹き込んだことであろう。彼らは価値観と創作主題を共有することで結びついていた。彼らが個人的に経験した緊張・困難はグループ内からではなく外部と状況から生じていた。繰り返しになるが、これは協働的思考と気の合う同士の議論の場であり、そこに立ち入れるほかの建築家はおらず、若いデザイナーであったマッキントッシュに自信を与えたに相違ない。

上記3つの協働は親密さと信頼に裏打ちされたものである。次に述べる協働は建築事務所で発生するであろう従来の協働であり、マッキントッシュが当時にしてこの場を創造的原動力と共同作業の機会として利用したという点で注目に値する。

ハニマン・アンド・ケペ：事務所
現在、建築事務所とは共同作業の場でありそこでつくられるものは潜在的に共同作品であると考えられている。たった一人の人間の働きによって建物が実現することなどほとんどなく、成果物を事務所や個人の名義にすることはできても、一つの建築物の実現に関与する相互作用を正確に描写することはめったにない。事務所を通じて、関係者は資源・経験・前例を共有する。これは受動ではなく能動的プロセスである。ハニマン・アンド・ケペは、事務所内で様々なアイディアを様式的に追求できるようにしつつも、なおも同一の事務所としての作家性を共有していたように見える。ハニマン・アンド・ケペは専門的事務所として正統的であろうとした一方で、マッキントッシュを鍛錬したのは、何年にもわたる見習い修行とグラスゴー美術学校での夜間授業であった[1]。事務所での経験により、マッキントッシュはグラスゴー美術学校の完成工事の休止期間中に、東西ファサードのデザインをラディカルに展開しつつも、全体の連続的統一感を保つことが可能であった。こうした進化は心変わりではなくデザイン思考の深化を示している。

クライアント：パトロンとユーザー
マッキントッシュとクライアントとのつながりと交流は、しばしば型にはまった関係性や役割の制限を超えた協働的対話となり、持続的かつ生産的に相互に敬意を払う関係性が生まれた。その結果、グラスゴー美術学校をはじめとしたプロジェクトのおかげで依頼が増加し、マッキントッシュは自分好みの作業方法を追求できるようになり、またデザインを進化させ新たな状況・発見・考察に対応できるようになった。ここでクライアントは報酬の支払源ではなく、協働的プロセスを通じてより多くを得ることのできるパトロンへと変身する。

これら創造的協働において、マッキントッシュは正統派空間と親密空間の間で活動をし、それによってもたらされる機会（およびリスク）が高まるなかで成長していったようだ。マッキントッシュは他者から影響を与えられたり、反対にに他者に影響を与えたりした。影響の広がりとこうしたインプットに対応する彼の用意周到さは、デザインをごく最終段階までオープンのままにしておくことで、彼の「習慣」の一部となり、個人的創造実践に組み込まれていた。それはユニークでなくとも彼の作品にとってはは根本的なことであり、結果として得られた統合はグラスゴー美術学校のデザインに明らかであり、関連性を残す寄与因子となっている。

サリー・スチュワート
（松本晴子訳）

Notes:
1. Mackintosh completed his 5-year apprenticeship in the office of John Hutchison in 1889, before he moved to Honeyman and Keppie.

原註：
1. マッキントッシュは1889年にジョン・ハッチソンの事務所で5年間の修行を終え、その後ハニマン・アンド・ケペの事務所に移っている。

Exhibition Settings by The Four

ザ・フォーによる展示しつらえ

Two exhibitions of applied art in Vienna and Turin in the early 1900s, crucial to the disucssion of how Charles Rennie Mackintosh was received in continental Europe, also provide insight into the beginning of a collaborative relationship of the quartet known as The Glasgow Four, and their practice.

Mackintosh, the sisters Margaret and Frances Macdonald, and James Herbert MacNair met as fellow students at the Glasgow School of Art in the mid-1890s, and it was the school director at the time, Francis Newbery, who brought them together. Seeing affinities in their work, Newbery encouraged these young artists to work with each other.[1] By 1895, the public had come to recognize the 4 artists as a cohesive group, and an arts and crafts exhibition held by Newbery that year featured works by the MacDonald sisters and MacNair consisting of a decorative mirror and screen. Despite the fact that Mackintosh did not exhibit there, their 4 names were mentioned side by side in the exhibition reviews. In 1899, the MacDonald sisters exhibited a series of works on the theme of the 4 seasons (each sister addressing 2 seasons, individually signed) at the Second Exhibition of The International Society of Sculptors, Painters and Gravers in London. Although they did not collaborate on any other works, the 4 artists were referred to together as a "quartet" due to their common style, which later came to be known as the Glasgow style.

Secession Exhibition at the Turn of the Century
The turn of the century brought changes to the relationship between the four. In 1899, Frances and Herbert MacNair married and moved to Liverpool, and the following year, in August 1900, Charles Mackintosh and Margaret Macdonald became husband and wife. In July that same year, they received a letter from Carl Moll, the president of the Vienna Secession at the time. It was an official invitation to the Eighth Exhibition of the Vienna Secession, which was being prepared to be held in November that year. Vienna Secessionist such as Josef Hoffmann had already been influenced by the paintings of Glasgow School, which had been exhibited in Vienna several years earlier to great acclaim. And this invitation came after Fritz Waerndorfer, a Secession patron, had visited England and Glasgow at Hoffmann's request. The press release of this Secession exhibition was the first mention of the collaboration of these 4 artists as a quartet: the beginning of The Four's shared production.[2]

The Scottish section of the Eighth Exhibition was located in Hall 10 (Saal X), in the east corner of Secession Building, designed by Joseph Maria Olbrich. This Secession exhibition was the first exhibition to focus mainly on crafts and was intended to juxtapose the achievements of craft reforms in other countries with those in their own. Unlike the subsequent exhibition in Turin, Mackintosh did not exhibit the room itself, choosing instead to design an installation comprised of mainly white panels to serve as a backdrop for the exhibits. It was here that 33 works by The Four – furniture, metalwork, glass, plaster panels, and so on – were displayed. Two gesso panel series,

The May Queen by Margaret and *The Wassail* by Mackintosh, were displayed at a certain height, and were particularly eye-catching. Originally commissioned by Catherine Cranston to decorate her Ingram Street Tea Rooms (p. 107), these 2 works were hung opposite each other on the upper wall of White Dining Room. Although little documentation remains of the Mackintosh couple's collaboration, a letter from Mackintosh to a friend indicates that they "worked together" on these 2 works.[3] The Four's exhibition attracted a great deal of both attention and criticism. Although the preface to the catalog stated that the purpose of the exhibition was "not showing interiors . . . but single pieces as samples of the various designers," many references were made to the magical atmosphere of the Scottish Room that was filled with The Four's work. Reviewers noted the sense of stylistic unity that dominated this white room, and questioned the nature of its authorship.

***The Rose Boudoir* in Turin**
Following the success of the Secession exhibition, the next stage for The Four in continental Europe was the First International Exhibition of Modern Decorative Arts, held in Turin in 1902. Thanks to Newbery, representing Scotland, a total of more than 50 artist were exhibited, and Mackintosh was charged with the design of the 3 rooms assigned to the Scottish section. The first room, painted in silver, white, and rose, was devoted to works by Mackintosh and Margaret: selections from a portfolio of House for an Art Lover (pp. 66–71), and a room arrangement called *The Rose Boudoir*. The next room showcased the MacNairs' study in white and gray-gold, while the last room in white and gold-purple showcased exhibits on display shelves designed by Mackintosh. On display as part of the Mackintoshes' *The Rose Boudoir* were 2 series of gesso panels by Margaret, *The White Rose and the Red Rose* and *The Heart of the Rose*, 3 white high-back chairs and an oval table by Mackintosh, and a writing desk fitted with 3 small plaster panels by Margaret and designed by Mackintosh. According to a review in *Studio* magazine, this room was "the 'clou' of the Scottish section . . . an epitome of the work of an architect and of an art-worker, laboring together as co-partners in the same scheme."[4]

Their exhibitions in continental Europe that began at the turn of the century went on to be held in Dresden, Berlin, and Moscow, and The Four, especially the Mackintoshes, worked actively in various locations until around 1906, and the acquaintances they made on the continent continued. In 1903, at the time of the founding of Wiener Werkstätte, Mackintosh, through Waerndorfer, wrote to Hoffman and Koloman Moser, encouraging them to pursue their visions. The works by these artists displayed at these venues, while individually belonging to each artist, were at their best when they were created as part of a collaborative setting, producing a perfect sense of aesthetic harmony and unity as a whole.

Translated by Darryl Jingwen Wee

チャールズ・レニー・マッキントッシュの大陸欧州での受容を語るにあたって肝要とされる2つの展覧会、1900年代初頭に開催されたウィーンとトリノにおける応用芸術の展示からは、ザ・フォーと呼ばれた四人組の協働関係の始まりとその実践も読み解くことができる。

マッキントッシュ、マーガレットとフランシスのマクドナルド姉妹、ジェームズ・ハーバート・マクネイアーの4名は1890年台の半ば、グラスゴー美術学校の学生時代に出会っている。4名を引き合わせたのは当時の校長、フランシス・ニューベリーであった。彼らによる作品に似通ったものを見出したニューベリーはこの若いアーティストらをうながし、ともに制作を行うことを勧めたという[1]。1895年になる頃には世間も4名をまとまりとして認識しており、その年にニューベリーによって開かれた美術工芸展では、マクドナルド姉妹とマクネイアーによる共著作品——装飾鏡と衝立——が出展され、この場へのマッキントッシュによる出展はなかったにもかかわらず、4名の名前は展覧会評において並んで記されている。1899年には、ロンドンで開かれた第2回国際彫刻家・画家協会展にマクドナルド姉妹による四季をテーマにした連作（2季づつにそれぞれが署名）が出展され、そのほかに協働作品はなかったにもかかわらず、4名は合わせて「カルテット」と呼ばれており、共通する——のちにグラスゴー・スタイルと呼ばれる——作風への言及がなされている。

世紀の変わりのウィーン分離派展

世紀の変わり目にあって、4名の関係にも変化が生じていた。1899年にはフランシスとマクネイアーが結婚しリバプールへと居を移しており、翌年の1900年8月にはマーガレットとマッキントッシュが夫婦となる。そして同年7月、ウィーン分離派の当時総裁カール・モルからの便りが届く。その年11月の開催へと準備が進められていた第8回分離派展への正式な招待状であった。ウィーン分離派のヨーゼフ・ホフマンらは既に数年前にウィーンで展示され大きな評判を博していたグラスゴー派の絵画に影響を受けており、これは分離派のパトロンであったフリッツ・ヴェルンドルファーがホフマンの頼みでグラスゴーを含めた英国を訪問した上での招待であった。この分離派展のリリースをもって、4名のアーティストの四人組としての協働にはじめての言及がなされている。ザ・フォーの「共同制作」[2]の始まりである。

第8回分離派展のスコットランド部門は、ヨゼフ・マリア・オルブリッヒ設計による分離派会館の東角、ホール10（Saal X）に位置していた。この分離派展は第8回にしてはじめて工芸品を主体とし、諸外国での工芸改革の成果と自国のそれとを併置して見せることを大きな目的としていた。後述のトリノとは異なり、ウィーンにおいてマッキントッシュは部屋のしつらえ自体の展示を行うことはなく、展示品の背景となる白を基調としたパネルのインスタレーションを設計、ここにザ・フォーによる作品——家具、金属加工品、ガラス、石膏パネルなど——全33点が出展された。高い位置に飾られ、とりわけ目を惹いたのが石膏パネルの2連作、マーガレットによる《The May Queen》とマッキントッシュによる《The Wassail》であった。元々この2作はキャサリン・クランストンから内装を依頼されたイングラム・ストリートのティールーム（107頁）のために制作され、店のホワイト・ダイニング・ルームの壁上方に向かい合って飾られていた。マッキントッシュ夫妻の協働を記す資料はほとんど残されていないが、マッキントッシュから友人へ宛てた手紙には、夫妻がこの2作品に「一緒にとり組んでいた」ことが記されている[3]。ザ・フォーによる展示は注目を集め、多くの批評が寄せられた。展覧会カタログの序文においては、当展の目的が「内装の展示ではなく（中略）様々なデザイナーによる作品の見本品を単品として見せること」にあると記されてはいたが、ザ・フォーの作品でうめられたスコットランド・ルームの幻想的な雰囲気への言及は多くなされている。評者らはこの白い部屋を圧倒的に占める様式的統一性をとりあげ、その創作者の所在を問うている。

トリノの《薔薇の私室》

分離派展の成功を受け、ザ・フォーにとって大陸欧州での次の舞台となったのが、1902年にトリノで開かれた現代装飾美術国際展示会であった。スコットランドの代表を務めたニューベリーを通し、総勢50名以上のアーティストが出展し、マッキントッシュはスコットランド部門に割り当てられた3部屋のデザインを任されている。銀・白・薔薇色で彩られた第一の部屋はマッキントッシュとマーガレットの作品——芸術愛好家の家（66〜71頁）のポートフォリオからの抜粋と《薔薇の私室（The Rose Boudoir）》と呼ばれた部屋のしつらえ——にあてられ、次の部屋は白・灰金色のマクネイアー夫妻による書斎のしつらえ、そして最後の白・金紫色の部屋にはマッキントッシュによる展示棚に飾られた出展物が並んでいた。マッキントッシュ夫妻による《薔薇の私室》の一環として展示されたのが、マーガレットによる2連の石膏パネル《The White Rose and the Red Rose》《The Heart of the Rose》、マッキントッシュによる白いハイバック・チェア2脚とオーヴァル・テーブル、そしてマッキントッシュがデザインしマーガレットによる3枚の小ぶりな石膏パネルがはめられた執筆机であった。『スタジオ』誌の批評をひくと、この部屋は「スコットランド部門の主眼であり、一つの構想を共有した建築家と美術工芸家間で行われるべく協働の鑑たる一例」[4]であったという。

世紀の変わり目から始まった彼らの大陸欧州での出展はその後ドレスデン、ベルリン、モスクワなどの地に続き、1906年ごろまでザ・フォー——特にマッキントッシュ夫妻は各地で活動的に仕事を行った。大陸で得た知己はその後も続き、1903年のウィーン工房設立の期にあたってマッキントッシュは、ヴェルンドルファーを通してホフマンとコロマン・モーザーに激励を記している。これらの会場に並べられた彼らの作品は、単体では各アーティストに属しつつも、協働の中で創出された場にあってこそ真骨頂を見せ、総体として完璧な美的調和と一体感を生みだしていた。

Notes:
1. Thomas Howarth, *Charles Rennie Mackintosh and the Modern Movement* (London: Routledge Kegan & Paul, 1952), p. 25.
2. Janice Helland, "Collaboration Amongst the Four," *Charles Rennie Mackintosh (Catalogue of the Exhibition)*, ed. Wendy Kaplan (London: Abbeville Press in association with Glasgow Museums, 1996).
3. Robyne Calvert, "The Künstlerpaar: Mackintosh, Macdonald & The Rose Boudoir," *Journal of the Charles Rennie Mackintosh Society* no. 102, p. 33.
4. "The First Exhibition of Modern Decorative Art at Turin – The Scottish Section," *Studio* no. 26, 1902, p. 96.

原註：英文参照。

a+u Digital Issues

2022年9月号
Grafton Architects
グラフトン・アーキテクツ

2022年8月号
6a architects
6aアーキテクツ

2022年7月号
Landscape Urbanism in France
フランスのランドスケープ・アーバニズム

2022年6月号
Christian Kerez
クリスチャン・ケレツ

2022年5月号
Francis Kéré
フランシス・ケレ

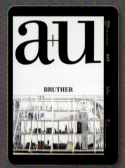
2022年4月号
BRUTHER
ブルーター

2022年3月号
Colombia
コロンビア

2022年2月号
Bernardo Bader
ベルナルド・バーダー

2022年1月号
Dwelling Studies and Japan's Women Architects
住居学と日本の女性建築家

2021年12月号
Paulo Mendes da Rocha
パウロ・メンデス・ダ・ローシャ

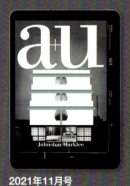
2021年11月号
Johnston Marklee
ジョンストン・マークリー

2021年10月号
Marie-José Van Hee architecten
マリー・ジョゼ・ヴァン・ヒ・アルキテクテン

We are on Zinio!
電子書籍発売中

日本国内からのご購入は：japan-architect.co.jp
海外からの購入は：au-magazine.com

zinioサイトでのご購入となります
zinioをはじめてご利用の方は、ユーザー登録が必要となります
目次リンク、頁リンク機能付き（広告など一部頁を除いております）